RTA Allegations of Fraud in a Post-Jackson Era: The Handbook 2nd Edition

Andrew Mckie,
Barrister at Law, Clerksroom (Manchester),
LLB Hons, PG DIP and
Former Solicitor Advocate,
Personal Injury, Fraud, Credit Hire

Law Brief Publishing

Published 2016 by
Law Brief Publishing
30 The Parks
Minehead
Somerset
TA24 8BT

www.lawbriefpublishing.com

Paperback: 978-1-911035-01-5

PREFACE

The Law of Personal Injury Insurance Fraud is a rapidly expanding area of practice, and the law is ever changing in this area. The ABI's 2012 statistics show that the total value of detected fraud for non-life insurance in 2012 exceeded £1bn for the first time.[1]

Allegations of fraud in road traffic claims, are not new. The practice of alleging fraud in such cases go back to the mid nineties and perhaps before. However, it was approaching the turn of the millennium it seems that law firms started to make this a specialist area of practice. It seems now that almost every insurer has an 'insurance fraud team' or a 'claims validation team', and similarly most of the large insurance based law firms have some kind of specialist practice in insurance fraud, with a specialised group of practitioners, dedicated to the subject.

According to the Insurance Fraud Bureau, undetected general insurance claims fraud totals £2.1 billion per year, adding on average £50 to the annual costs individual policyholders face each year.[2] The IFB further estimates that 1 in 7 personal injury claims are linked to 'cash for crash' scams, £392 million is the annual cost of 'cash for crash' fraud, and 84% of motorists are concerned about the rising cost of insurance premiums to cover the costs of fraud.[3]

It is little wonder therefore, that over the last few years claimant law firms have become increasingly interested in trying to eliminate this type of fraud from their case loads, and increasingly are setting up specialist teams to deal with such cases, that require specialist knowledge.

The aim of this book is to provide a clear but comprehensive guide to this ever changing area of practice, that can be utilised by practitioners on a day-to-day basis, in claimant and defendant practice. It seems there are few

---

1 https://www.abi.org.uk/News/Industry-data-updates/2013/07/Detected-fraud-statistics-update

2 http://www.insurancefraudbureau.org

3 http://view.digipage.net/?userpath=00000817/00017508/00080957/

dedicated texts that practitioners can use on a day-to-day basis in practice, on this subject.

This 2016 second edition has been fully updated from the first edition to include:

- Fundamental Dishonesty and Section 57 Update and relevant cases.
- The Recent Cases surrounding QOCS and QOCS update including section 57 fundamental dishonesty.
- Hayward v Zurich and reopening concluded settlements.
- LVI – a more rigorous approach to litigation.
- The decision is Qader v Esure/ Broadhurst v Tan and Costs Implications for Alleged Fraud cases.
- An analysis of the future of fraud litigation in practice.
- Updates on fraud cases and pleadings.
- Committal proceedings (an update).

The book will aim to cover most areas of personal injury insurance fraud, and in particular focuses on the day-to-day issues in practice, one encounters with such cases.

I would encourage the reader to 'dip in and out' of the book as and when required.

I wish to thank Tim Kevan of Law Brief Publishing for providing me with the opportunity to write this book, and the PI Brief Update website for publishing relevant sections.

Andrew Mckie
Fraud and Personal Injury Barrister
August 2016

Contents

CHAPTER ONE
LOW VELOCITY IMPACTS: AN UPDATE 2016

What is a Low Velocity Impact?

A low velocity impact is commonly defined as a road traffic collision where it is alleged by the Defendant's insurer that the impact is unlikely to have caused injury to the Claimant, due to the low speed of the impact, and/or, that there was sufficient occupant displacement within the vehicle, in order to have caused injury to the Claimant.

Low velocity impacts are probably one of the most common types of alleged fraud, and appear most frequently in cases involving alleged fraud, hence a whole chapter has been dedicated to the issue of low velocity type impacts in this book. Typically low speed impacts or low velocity impacts as they are sometimes known, are one of the most difficult alleged frauds to investigate. Almost always, the success or failure of the case at Trial, will almost wholly depend upon the credibility of the Claimant.

This chapter is entirely dedicated to low velocity/low speed impacts for that reason and the chapter is focussed upon the investigation of low speed impacts for Claimant and Defendant practitioners, and additionally to resolve cases effectively and efficiently.

Spotting the Warning Signs

Some of the commonly defined features of a low velocity type impact maybe as follows:-

(a) The Defendant's insurer says that the damage to the insured vehicle was minimal.

(b) The damage to the Claimant's vehicle was minimal.

(c) The Defendant's insured describes the impact as less than five miles per hour, or perhaps even slower.

(d) Examination of the damage to both vehicles and the photographs or engineering evidence shows little or no damage to either vehicle.

(e) The parties describe the impact as low speed or very light.

(f) The Defendant's insured says that he was not moved within his seat, or restrained by the seatbelt and no items were displaced in the Defendant's insured vehicle.

(g) The Claimant's vehicle was not shunted or moved by the impact in any way.

(h) The Claimant says that he was not restrained by his seatbelt.

It may be that one of the above features may indicate that a claim was a low velocity type impact or collision and it may be that that these features may lead to an investigation as such.

Engineering Evidence

The use of engineering evidence can be extremely useful in low velocity impact type cases. An automotive assessor's report and photographs of the damage to both vehicles will enable one to assess the following information:-

1. The damage to the respective vehicles and exactly how much damage was caused to both vehicles.

2. Areas of damage to both vehicles – are they consistent?

3. The parts that required replacement on both vehicles.

4. The labour and repair costs for both vehicles.

However, when assessing the level of damage to both vehicles, one should be careful not to solely base the investigation upon engineering evidence as it can be misleading in certain circumstances, as to the extent of the impact between the vehicles. Insurance companies for example in some circumstances can allege that a case is a low velocity impact, solely based upon the lack of damage to the vehicles.

However, commonly in some instances, the Defendant's engineer will not inspect behind the bumper of the Defendant's insured vehicle, to check if there is any damage behind the bumper, for example to the bumper reinforcer or steel bar behind the bumper. The structure of modern day road traffic collision investigation, often dictates that automotive assessments, as opposed to forensic engineering assessments, take place either via desktop enquiries, or very quick inspections of the Defendant's insured vehicle without taking it into a garage to remove the bumper. If the Defendant's insurer alleges that the collision is a low velocity one, one should be careful to check that the Defendant's insurer has instructed the automotive investigator to check for damage behind the bumper to the reinforcer bar, and if the reinforcer bar has sustained damage, it would indicate that this is a much stronger impact, than perhaps anticipated in the first instance.

Similarly, one could instruct the Claimant's engineer to check for damage behind the bumper in order to check the damage to the reinforcer bar or boot floor of the Claimant's vehicle, if it has been struck in the rear, which is often the common scenario in low velocity impact type cases. It is sometimes the case that the modern construction of vehicles means that bumpers made of plastic components are designed to flex and reflex at very low speed impacts i.e. less than five miles per hour and in some circumstances, even if there is damage behind the bumper it will not necessarily reflect by simply looking at the bumpers of the respective vehicles.

Forensic Engineering Evidence

It could be argued, that forensic engineering evidence is not always useful in low velocity or low speed impact type cases. The predominant reason for this, is that typically forensic engineers in this area have tended to stray into the realms of whether there was occupant displacement in the vehicle or not at certain speeds and arguments over Delta V, whether the Claimant could have sustained injury at certain speeds. It may be argued, that there is nothing wrong in practice in obtaining a forensic engineer's report, providing that the engineer solely focusses upon the damage that was sustained to the vehicles as a result of the collision, and particularly if it is alleged by the Defendant's insured, that some of the damage to the Claimant's vehicle was pre existing and/or was not caused as a result of the accident.

In the circumstances, it may be argued that a forensic engineer's report can be extremely useful in looking at the damage to the respective vehicles to determine what damage was caused as a result of the accident. Often the Defendant's insured will contend that all of the damage to the Claimant's vehicle was caused as a result of a previous collision.

Sometimes a forensic engineer's report, can also be useful in circumstances where a more detailed inspection is required of the damage to the respective vehicles. Often Courts are now prepared to accept the evidence of forensic engineers, who have not actually inspected the vehicles but have been able to prepare a report, on the basis of clear colour photographs of the damage to the respective vehicles. With the aid of modern technology, such as iPhones, iPads and digital cameras, this has become increasingly more economical and efficient. However, the photographs obtained of the vehicles must be entirely clear in colour and in a digital format, so that the engineer can prepare a full and credible report.

Casey –v- Cartwright

The case of *Debbie Casey –v- David Cartwright* was a 2006 Court of Appeal decision EWCA Civ 1280. In *Casey,* the Court of Appeal set out the guidance in relation to dealing with case management decisions and the need for expert evidence in low velocity impact type cases and it said:-

"We think that it is desirable that if a Defendant wishes to raise the causation issue, he should satisfy certain formalities. In this way the risk of confusion and delay to the proceedings should be minimised. Accordingly, where in a particular case the Defendant wishes to raise causation issue, he should notify all other parties in writing that he considers it to be a low velocity impact case and that he intends to raise the causation issue. For the reasons set out at paragraph 33 below, he should do so within three months of receipt of the Letter of Claim. The issue should be expressly identified in the Defence, supported in the usual way by a Statement of Truth. Within 21 days of serving a Defence raising the causation issue, the Defendant should serve upon the Court and the other parties a Witness Statement which clearly identifies the grounds upon which the issue is raised. Such a Witness Statement should be expected to deal with the Defendant's evidence relating to the issue, including the circumstances of the impact and the result of damage.

Upon receipt of a Witness Statement, the Court will, if satisfied that the issue has been properly identified and raised, generally give permission for the Claimant to be examined by a medical expert nominated by the Defendant.

If upon receipt of any medical evidence served by the Defendant following such examination the Court is satisfied on the entirety of the evidence submitted by the Defendant that he has properly identified the case upon the causation issue which has a real prospect of success, the Court will generally give the Defendant permission to rely upon such evidence.

We believe that what we have said reflects the tenor of the Judgment in Kearsley. There will however be circumstances where the Judge decides that, even though the evidence submitted by the Defendant shows that his case on causation has real prospects of success, the overriding objective nevertheless requires permission for expert evidence to be refused. It is not possible or desirable to produce an exhaustive list of such circumstances. They include the

> *following. First, the timing of the notification by the Defendant that he intends to raise the causation issue. Unless the Defendant notifies the Claimant of its intention to raise the issue within three months of receipt of the Letter of Claim, permission to rely upon expert evidence should usually be denied to the Defendant. It is important that the issue be raised at an early stage so as to avoid causing delay to the prosecution of the proceedings. The period of three months is consistent with paragraph 2.11 of the Pre-Action Protocol for personal injury claims which provides that a Defendant be given three months to investigate and respond to a claim before proceedings are issued.*
>
> *Secondly, if there is a single factual dispute the resolution of which one way or the other is likely to resolve the causation issue, this is a factor which militates against the granting of permission to rely upon expert evidence on the causation issue. In such a case, the expert evidence is likely to serve little or no purpose.*
>
> *Thirdly, there may be cases where the alleged injury and the damages claimed are so small and the nature of the evidence that the Defendant wishes to adduce is so extensive and complex the consideration and proportionality demand that permission on the evidence should be refused. This must be left to the good sense of the Judge. It does not detract from the general guidance given at paragraph 32 above"*

Given the guidance set out above, it can be argued that is still good law today, and if the Defendant has not followed the guidance set out in *Casey,* the Claimant's Solicitor should ordinarily object to the Defendant's insurer obtaining and relying upon its own Orthopaedic evidence. Similarly, given the limited time periods in *Casey*, it is essential, that the Defendant's insurer identifies low speed impact type cases as early on in the investigation process as possible, and clearly puts the Claimant's Solicitors on notice in writing, within three months of the Letter of Claim that causation is an issue and it is safer, from the point of view of *Casey,* to ensure that the Claimant's Solicitor is put on notice that the case is being investigated as a low velocity type impact.

However, post Jackson and in a fixed costs regime, it has to be said that very few insurers now seek to obtain their own expert evidence, so the point is now it can be argued largely redundant.

Disclosure of Medical Records

The case of *Kearsley –v- Klarfield 2005 EWCA Civ 1510*, makes it clear that in low velocity impact cases, the Claimant's advisers are advised to offer the Defendant's insurers access to the Claimant's vehicle for the purpose of early examination and give early disclosure of any contemporaneous GP or other relevant medical notes to enable the Defendant's insurers to obtain the relevant material expeditiously and inexpensively. Again, this is still good law, and where a low velocity impact is alleged, the Defendant's insurer could obtain early disclosure from the Claimant or relevant General Practitioner and hospital notes.

It may also be advisable for Claimant Lawyers at an early stage to peruse the Claimant's medical records and hospital notes as soon as the issue of causation is raised in a low velocity type impact, to confirm whether the Claimant's instructions concerning injuries, attendances at the hospital, attendances at the General Practitioner, effect on lifestyle, work and home, are consistent with what the Claimant told the medical expert, and also the instructing Solicitor.

It may be argued, that if the Claimant's evidence is inconsistent at Trial between his hospital notes, General Practitioner records, his Witness Statements and his medical report, it will more often than not lead to the case failing upon the issue of causation at Trial. For example see *John Paul Humphries –v- Jonathan Matthews 2006.* This case involved Mr Humphries seeking damages for loss and injury he claims to have suffered as a consequence of a low velocity rear end impact to the motor vehicle he was driving on 09 February 2005. The Defendant admitted the collision, but contended that the vehicles only "kissed" very lightly. Recorder Andrew G Moran QC on 16 June 2006 stated:

> *"Having given careful consideration to all of the arguments at every stage, I have come to the sure conclusions previously expressed. To*

the same standard, as in all of my following conclusions, I am satisfied that the Claimant has sought to obtain for himself a lump sum of money by deception being aware of the fact that insurers commonly pay out in cases without testing the evidence. He did not bank on the strong perception of anticipated injustice that his behaviour would engender in Mr Matthews, who as I find, with no motive whatsoever to serve for himself, was immediately determined the Claimant was not going to get away with what I find he threatened to do.

The arguments to that effect that if the Claimant had been intent on fraud he would have realised that or acted differently, are completely overwhelmed by the compelling evidence of what he did not do and say and what he did not report so that I am left with no doubt about his intentions from the moment when he could not procure enough by way of cash from Mr Matthews to satisfy him.

I am satisfied that there was no injury or any aggravation of a pre-existing condition in this very minor impact.

I am satisfied that the Claimant first tried to get money out of Mr Matthews and did say "make me an offer" when there was no acceptable offer was forthcoming, he was determined to make a false whiplash claim and threatened to take Mr Matthews to the cleaners. I am consequently satisfied that he had lied to me on oath in denying those things in his evidence before me. I am satisfied that those lies were not told innocently to avoid having to concede disgraceful behaviour but were told in furtherance of this dishonest scheme.

I am satisfied that following a course of action involving the required logging of a claim with a GP. The purpose of his attendance to seek medical help for an injury sustained but to tick one of the boxes in pursuit of a personal injury claim.

I am satisfied that his failure to respond honestly and truthfully, fully and accurately to Dr Hershon's obvious questions about his past medical history was deliberate and contrived so as to prevent his claim for a whiplash injury as the effect of a rear end shunt. This was to avoid the complication he well understood would arise of prompting an insurer to closer scrutiny of his claim if he revealed this was his third whiplash claim in under ten years and he had a troublesome pre existing spinal disorder.

As in all detected frauds there were things he did not bargain for including the prospect and effect of Dr Hershon's review of his medical records and his retraction of his prognosis. He was then forced to shift his ground to present his case on a different basis. He has been found out by the honesty and integrity of Mr Matthews and his insurer's willingness to stand and fight a false claim.

This claim is dismissed with costs on a basis to be determined".

This case, opened the ground for the Defendant's Counsel to make an Application for referral of the papers to the Attorney General and/or the Chief Constable of the Police force who had jurisdiction for that part of the country where the collision occurred for consideration of a criminal investigation.

Previous Medical Reports

It may be prudent to ask the Claimant at the outset of the case, details of all of the previous road traffic accidents that he has ever been involved in, whether as a result of being a driver, passenger and regardless of whether a claim was made or not. It can be argued, that one of the most common reasons low velocity impact claims fail at Trial is because the Claimant has failed to disclose such accidents either deliberately or innocently to the medical expert. From a Claimant's perspective, if the Claimant is put on notice that the Defendant's insurer is investigating the matter as a low velocity impact type collision, it is advisable that all of the Claimant's GP and hospital notes are obtained prior to instruction of the medical expert, and the Claimant's expert has these for the purpose of the examination.

The Claimant's Solicitor may want to satisfy himself in terms of the prospect of success of the case, that the Claimant has disclosed all previous accidents involving injury or not regardless or whether a claim was made, at the outset of the case. If the Claimant has failed to disclose previous accidents or injuries to either the Claimant's Solicitor or the medical expert, then detailed instructions may be taken from the Claimant as to why, and in the absence of a credible explanation, one may wish to question why the Claimant has withheld such information.

The same may equally apply in relation to previous injuries or whiplash type injuries sustained by the Claimant in similar areas or to similar parts of the body in previous collisions, or entirely separate accidents. Full scrutiny of the General Practitioner records and hospital records will often reveal whether the Claimant has been forthright with his own Solicitors. It can be argued that one would question the credibility of a Claimant who has failed to disclose a number of previous road traffic accidents to either his Solicitors, the Defendant or his own medical expert, or a Claimant who has withheld the history of previous back or neck problems in a whiplash type claim, particularly if the Claimant has been involved in previous medical examinations for road traffic accidents, prior to the accident that the Claimant's Solicitor is dealing with.

It may be that the Claimant's Solicitor will also want to check, if the Claimant has been involved in previous road traffic accidents, and copies of those medical reports may need to be obtained, to check whether the Claimant has been forthright, with the previous medical experts. If not, the Claimant may be carefully questioned as to why not.

It may equally apply for any subsequent road traffic accidents that the Claimant has been involved in following the road traffic accident in question. If there are subsequent medical reports, one could check the subsequent medical reports to ensure that the index accident and injuries were mentioned to the subsequent medical experts. The Court is likely to be very sceptical of any Claimant who has failed to mention previous or subsequent road traffic accidents or injuries, particularly if that Claimant has been involved in a number of previous whiplash claims or medical examinations.

It is a sad fact of modern road traffic accident litigation that many medical examinations are carried out quickly and is arguable that in some instances, it is questionable whether the medical expert asks all of the correct questions of the Claimant in medical examinations. It is particularly the case, it can be argued where cases are being dealt with initially in the low value road traffic portal and the existence of pro-forma medical reports, which are to some extent a tick box exercise.

If the first medical report has been produced in such circumstances in the low value road traffic portal, it is prudent that the medical report is sent to the Claimant, by the Claimant's Solicitor to be thoroughly checked for accuracy before it is disclosed to the Defendant's insurer. It may further assist if the Claimant Lawyer goes through the entirety of the medical report over the telephone with the Claimant to ensure the documents factual accuracy, before it is disclosed. If a report has been created in the low value portal, without reference to medical records, that an addendum report may be obtained with full medical records review including General Practitioner and hospital records, if the Defendant's insurer has put the Claimant's Solicitor on notice that the claim is being investigated as a low velocity impact type collision.

One should be particularly careful with Claimants whose first language is not English. Sometimes, there are cases where medical examinations have been conducted in English where the Claimant either has a poor grasp of the English language, or has not been able to understand all of the questions in the examination due to language difficulties and mis-understanding of English words. If the Claimant has a poor grasp of English, or there is a language barrier, it may be prudent for the Claimant to either have an independent interpreter to assist at the medical examination, or the Claimant could be sent to a medical examiner, who can conduct the medical examination and interview in the Claimant's own language.

If the Claimant does not speak English or read and write English, the medical report could be translated into the Claimant's own language, and sent to the Claimant to read and check before it is disclosed by the Defendant's insurers. There are some instances where the above has not carried out which can sometimes lead to inaccuracies or inconsistencies in the medical report which are not due to credibility, but are due to language barriers and correct and/or lack of interpretation or translation.

If the Claimant does not read or write English, it may be that before the medical report is disclosed to the Defendant's insurer, it is extremely useful if the Claimant's Solicitor either instructs an independent interpreter, or has the relevant fee earner read over the medical report to the Claimant in his own language and signs the correct translation certificate to ensure that the Claimant has fully understood the document before it is disclosed.

Modern road traffic law, and the introduction of fixed fees into the road traffic portal, which in July 2013 were reduced even further, means that the practicalities of translation and the like can sometimes make these matters more difficult. However, it can be argued, that if Claimants' Solicitors pursue such claims, it is prudent that translation of documents are provided to Claimants, to ensure the effective running of the case and to discharge the duty of care to the Claimant

Seeking Disclosure of CUE Searches

The CUE database or the Claims and Underwriting Exchange is a central database of motor, home and personal injury incidents reported to insurance companies which may or may not give rise to a claim. The CUE underwriting database has been in existence since 1994 and there are currently 99 subscribers to CUE including 60 insurers, 30 other authorised members and 9 associated members. It can be found at: www.insurancedatabases.co.uk

Insurers exchange information with each other concerning previous claims histories for any claims reported to them by the Claimant or policyholder involving either the incident in question or other road traffic accidents or insurance claims. More often than not, the insurance company to which the claim is submitted, will have access to the CUE database, and it is more likely than not that the Defendant's insurer will know about the Claimant's previous claims history and any inconsistencies in the medical report.

The Claimant's Solicitor, is able to access a copy of the same information by asking the Claimant to fill in the subject access request form which can be found at www.insurancedatabases.co.uk and sending the SAR form to the Insurance Database Services Limited with a cheque for £10 to the following address Insurance Database Services Limited, Risk & Compliance, Linford Wood House, 6–12 Capital Drive, Milton Keynes, MK4 6XT. This will give the Claimant access to any information held upon the database any incidents or claims.

In the alternative, the Claimant's Lawyer can ask the Defendant's insurer or Solicitor for disclosure of the CUE searches, but the Defendant's insurer is unlikely to provide disclosure of the relevant searches, until the Claimant has answered Part 18 Questions with a Statement of Truth for obvious reasons. It is therefore advisable, that if you are a Claimant's Solicitor to obtain a copy of the Claimant's history by filling in the subject access form and sending it to CUE, to get a full copy of the Claimant's claim history, at the outset of the claim via the subject access request form. It is clear that the subject access request form, must be completed and signed by the Claimant however, and it cannot be signed or completed by the Claimant's Solicitor.

Low Velocity Impact Claims – Why Do They Fail At Trial?

It is submitted, that these types of claims commonly fail at Trial, ultimately due to the Claimant's credibility or lack of it. The credibility of the Claimant may be undermined by the Defendant's insurer, with reference to claims history, failure to disclose previous accidents, the Claimant being unable to confirm when he first experienced pain due to his or her whiplash injuries, inconsistencies in the reporting of the accident and symptoms to the General Practitioner or hospital Consultant, inconsistencies in relation to how the injury was caused in the first instance and the mechanism of the accident i.e. did the Claimant go forwards and backwards or side to side in the seat, inconsistencies in relation to the amount of damage that was caused to the vehicle, the inconsistencies in relation to how far the Claimant's vehicle was shunted in the collision.

Sometimes, when an allegation of a low velocity impact is put to the Claimant, one might see that the Claimant begins to embellish or exaggerate certain parts of the factual mechanism of the accident or injury. For example the Claimant may initially say that the vehicle was not shunted in the accident, but when one tells the Claimant that the claim is being investigated as a low velocity impact, the Claimant may say that the vehicle was in fact shunted a few feet, or suggest that the damage was much more severe than when instructions were initially taken. The Claimant's Solicitor can be aware of this, and question the credibility of a Claimant who chooses to exaggerate the speed, factual mechanism of the accident or injury. This is unlikely to come across well in Court it is submitted.

A credible Claimant is simply a Claimant who is telling the truth. In alleged fraud cases, it is always useful to call the Claimant into the office to go through the factual circumstances of the accident and the mechanism of injury, and if that is not possible at the very least a Conference by telephone with Counsel. Watch out for the body language of the Claimant during the interview. Is the Claimant nervous? Do they maintain eye contact? Are they fidgety? When taking into account the Claimant may be nervous about attending upon the Solicitor for interview, these are all telltale signs something may not be quite right.

Almost all low velocity impact Trials are won or lost upon the credibility of the Claimant and how well the Claimant will present in the witness box. It is always prudent to invite the Claimants to interview or Conference with Counsel to test the credibility of the Claimants' version prior to Trial. This is especially important given the potential for referral to the Crown Prosecution Service or proceedings for contempt of Court in the event that the Claimant is found to have misled the Court in the witness box and/or verified Statements of Truth which the Claimant knows to be false.

The burden is upon the Claimants to prove the case on the balance of probability. A Claimant whose case has lots of inconsistencies, which cannot be explained in relation to either factual or medical causation, is a case that may be in difficulty at the final Trial of the matter. It is therefore essential, that the Claimant's Solicitor knows the Claimant's case inside out, and what the Claimant is likely to say in the witness box. Testing the Claimant's evidence in interview or Conference, should not be confused with coaching the witness. The proof of evidence is taken from the Claimant in a low velocity impact case, and any other road traffic accident for that matter, it is vitally important that the Claimant's evidence is taken in the Claimant's own words. A Witness Statement which is in a Lawyer's language, does not gain favour with the Judge.

Pre-Action Protocols

The Personal Injury Pre-Action Protocol for low value personal injury claims in road traffic accidents pre 31 July 2013 says in Section 6.15:-

> *"The claim will no longer continue under this protocol where the Defendant, within the period in paragraph 6.11 or 6.13 – makes an admission of liability but alleges contributory negligence (other than in relation to the Claimant's admitted failure to wear a seatbelt)"*

The protocol further says at paragraph 1.32 of the protocol that the claim will no longer continue under the protocol at stage 2, where the Defendant gives notice to the Claimant within the initial consideration period that the Defendant withdraws an admission of causation.

It is therefore arguable, that low velocity impact type allegations are unlikely to continue within the portal, since an admission in the portal requires an admission of breach of duty and an admission that the Defendant caused some loss or damage to the Claimant. A withdrawal of an admission or of causation, or not admitting causation, means that it is likely the Claimant will need to be required to attend Court on the issues of factual and medical causation, together with the Defendant's policyholder and therefore means that the claim is unsuitable for the low value portal.

If the claim exits the low value portal it will fall into the former Pre-Action Protocol for personal injury claims and it is submitted that in particular the following paragraphs are relevant:-

(a) 3.10 which says "*if the Defendant denies liability, he should enclose with the letter of reply documents in its possession which are material to the issues between the parties and which would be likely to be ordered to be disclosed by the Court, either on an Application for a Pre-Action Disclosure, or on disclosure during proceedings*".

(b) Pre-Action Personal Injury Protocol standard disclosure – fast track disclosure, suggests that the following documents should be disclosed in Section A "*where liability is an issue:-*

> *(i) Documents identifying the nature, extent and location of the damage to the Defendant's vehicle where there is any dispute about point of impact.*"

It is arguable, that this should include, the Defendant's engineering evidence and photographs if there is an argument in relation to causation or the nature and extent of the damage to either vehicle.

The Claimant's Solicitor may wish to consider an Application for Pre-Action Disclosure of these documents, in the event of non compliance by the Defendant's insurer, with reference to the following arguments:-

(a) It will save time and costs of litigation by disclosure of the documents; and

(b) The disclosure of the documents is relevant to the consistency and extent of damage to both vehicles where factual and medical causation is in dispute between the parties.

Obtaining Evidence To Support The Claimant's Case

In a low velocity impact type collision, it be extremely important that the Claimant's Solicitor obtains evidence to support the Claimant's case, particularly in relation to the issue of medical causation and this may include as follows:-

(a) The Claimant's physiotherapy records, to confirm the attendance at physiotherapy.

(b) Employment records to confirm the Claimant's absence from work, or a letter from the Claimant's employer to confirm the absence and the reason for the absence.

(c) Gym records or other sporting records if the Claimant has been away from sporting activities or leisure activities, or a Witness Statement to the same effect from the gym or the sports team.

(d) If the Claimant has also brought a claim for gratuitous care and assistance, a Witness Statement will also be required from the person who provided the care and assistance to the Claimant.

It may be that all of these documents can be incredibly useful when the Court makes a determination as to whether the Claimant was injured or not due to the road traffic collision and this is of particular importance if there is a claim for loss of earnings or the like, to provide support in relation to that aspect of the claim.

Sometimes one finds at Trial that these key documents are missing, particularly if the Claimant has advised the medical experts that there was an absence from work, he had physiotherapy, or did not attend the gym for a period of three months and it is easy to question the credibility of such claims, without the documentary evidence in support.

Golden –v- Dempsey

This claim related to an accident in December 2008 and the issue of LVI was raised within three months of the Letter of Claim. District Judge Holman in December 2010 provided some further guidance in relation to low velocity impact allegations and case management and in particular the conduct of the parties pre Trial. In this case the Claimant was ordered to pay the Defendant's costs of the Case Management Hearing, when ordinarily the Costs Order that would follow of such a hearing would be costs in the case and His Honour Judge Holman set out some of the reasons as follows:-

> *"The Court resources are scarce and in the near future will inevitably become scarcer still. With the disappearance of a designated Judge for the outer Manchester Courts, the burden of dealing with these cases have now fallen entirely on Manchester County Court. For reasons which are difficult to discern it is generally the case that little has been done to progress the claim after the Defence is served. The parties appear to prefer to wait until the inevitable first Directions Hearing. The resources that the hearing commonly takes longer and in some instances quite often as a consequence of an inadequate instruction to Counsel it proves impossible to make meaningful progress. The periods between causation being raised and the issue of the claim and between Defence and the first hearing, both of which could be used to good effect or wasted. If the parties adopted a proactive approach not only will the first hearing be speeded up, but it will also become more likely that the steps can be speeded up or at least delays can be reduced".*

His Honour Judge Holman further stated "*in the majority of cases it ought to be perfectly possible to have completed standard disclosure and inspection on a voluntary basis before the issue of proceedings and certainly before the first Directions Hearing*" with regards to the issues of medical records. It is clear, that *Golden –v- Dempsey* was a warning to Claimant and Defendant Lawyers who failed to engage in the issue of exchange of information and disclosure, prior to the first Directions Hearing.

LVI , QOCS and Section 57 Dishonesty (2016 Update)

Since 2013, it has arguably become more difficult to win alleged LVI cases at Trial, and there are many unreported cases by the insurers of LVI/causation disputes failing at trial and QOCS being dis-applied. The experience of Counsel is that now many cases which would have succeeded pre 2013, are now failing at Trial. In *Hughes, Kindon and Jones v KGM* (2016 unreported Taunton County Court), three claimants claimed they had suffered year-long injuries after an accident. A deputy district judge had rejected the contention that injuries persisted for 12 months in the case of two of the claimants, Hughes and Kindon, saying they were likely to have suffered for two weeks. The were initially awarded £750 each in damages. The court accepted the claims were fundamentally dishonest after the victims had stated during an examination six weeks after the accident they were still suffering from their injuries. Striking out the claims in their entirety, DDJ Eaton-Hart said the two claimants had '*presented a deliberate inaccurate position to the medical expert for financial gain*'. He also ruled that the claimants would not suffer substantial injustice from the decision. The claimants were ordered to pay £6,100 costs and were denied permission to appeal. QOCS and fundamental dishonesty will examined in more detail in later Chapters.

Summary

It is submitted, that low velocity impact type cases are extremely difficult for Claimant's Solicitors to win at Trial. Unless the Claimant's case is credible, with few inconsistencies, the case may be difficult to succeed on balance at Trial.

If the Defendant's insurer is given permission to access its own medical evidence, the Claimant's Lawyer can ensure that suitable Part 35 Questions are put to the medical expert to challenge any assertions that the Claimant could not have been injured as a result of the accident.

The Defendant's Lawyer on the other hand, will be keen to ensure that early Part 18 Questions are put to the Claimant, in order to clarify any inconsistencies in the evidence and particularly with regards to medical causation and previous accidents that the Defendant's insurer is aware that the Claimant has been involved in.

In modern day road traffic accident litigation, it may be essential that the Claimant's Solicitors meet the Claimant in person prior to Trial, to test the credibility of the Claimant's evidence and the reason for any inconsistencies, particularly with regards to previous road traffic collisions or previous injuries that are similar to ones involved in the index accident, given that it can be argued this is the reason that most claims fail at Trial.

CHAPTER TWO
STAGED/CONTRIVED ACCIDENTS: THE FRAUD OF CHOICE?

Spotting the Warning Signs

An alleged staged and/or contrived accident, may be defined as an attempt by an individual, or a group of individuals, in order to obtain monies either by submitting a claim to an insurance company for an accident which did not occur, ie a contrived accident, or deliberately crashing vehicles into each other on purpose, for the purposes of making claims for compensation.

There are a number of potential indicators of a staged and/or contrived accident and these may be broadly summarised as follows:-

(a) The policyholder's vehicle is of a low value.

(b) Multiple occupancy vehicles.

(c) The accident happens late at night or in a remote location.

(d) There are no Police, ambulance or attendance of the fire brigade.

(e) There are no witnesses to the accident or witnesses who can independently verify the circumstances of the accident.

(f) There are multiple personal injury claims from both vehicles.

(g) There may be the feature of a significant claim for credit hire, storage or vehicle damage, from the vehicle that has been struck.

(h) An uncooperative policyholder or a policyholder who does not respond to correspondence, phone calls or visits from his insurance company or who may not report the accident to his insurance company.

(i) Involvement of multiple accident management companies and/or claims companies.

(j) Inconsistent damage between the Claimant's vehicle and the policyholder's vehicle.

(k) Inconsistent versions of the accident circumstances from the various parties.

It may be argued that one or more of the above factors of a road traffic collision, may render the claim as one to investigate further for the Defendant's insurance company. The existence of such features of course, does not necessarily mean that there is anything untoward about the claim, but it may lead the Defendant's insurance company to cast further scrutiny on the claims as presented to them.

It is well known amongst the Claimant and Defendant communities, that road traffic insurers have systems in place either via computer systems and/or through human intervention, to pick out warning signs such as these in fraud prevention techniques. It may well be that these types of "fraud indicators" has led to an increase in the identification and detection of alleged fraudulent road traffic collisions by the insurance industry over the last ten years or so. This means that fraud prevention and detection facilities, continue to become ever more sophisticated as new technologies emerge.

The Importance of Vetting Procedures

Vetting procedures from both a Claimant and Defendant prospective, it may be argued are extremely important in any legal practice that is now engaged in personal injury litigation. Lawyers undertaking personal injury cases on a no win no fee basis, are particularly vulnerable to road traffic fraud, and especially those engaged in credit hire or claims management type work. It is therefore important that every practice has a robust system for identifying potentially fraudulent claims at the outset of the case and employing a system of fraud prevention, that can identify those types of cases that require further scrutiny and/or investigation. These types of investigations may involve either the Claimant, the policyholder, the circumstances of the accident, the hire company, storage company, or the accident management company and their involvement in relation to a claim.

With the emergence of high volume low cost driven personal injury litigation, it is submitted that it is even more important for even the most junior of fee earners to be alive to potentially fraudulent claims so these can be disposed of by the Claimant Lawyers at the earliest possible opportunity.

It is clear that fraudulent road traffic claims do not benefit anyone but the fraudsters themselves. The Defendant's insurers are forced to investigate claims running into many thousands of pounds and instructing Defendant Solicitors' firms to defend such cases, and Claimant Lawyers are left with costs bills on a conditional fee basis, that they are unable to enforce either against the Defendant through claims failing, and/or the Claimants themselves who engage in such activity who tend to disappear at the end of the case never to be seen again. It is clear therefore, that it is in everyone's interests to ensure that fraudulent claims are eliminated from personal injury litigation altogether at the earliest opportunity.

The following questions may be asked by the Claimant Lawyer at the outset of the case, in order to potentially detect a fraudulent claim which shows some or more of the above indicators:-

(a) Where were the Claimants going at the time of the accident?

(b) How do the Claimants know each other?

(c) Where had they all set off from and at what time?

(d) From where was the vehicle involved in the accident purchased and how long had the Claimant owned it?

(e) How much was the vehicle purchased for?

(f) What was the intended destination and who were the Claimants going to meet?

(g) Is there any evidence of who the Claimants were going to meet or the intended destination?

(h) Who was the Claimant's vehicle insured with, and for how long had it been insured with that insurance company?

If the Claimants are unable to answer the above questions, especially basic factual circumstances concerning the accident such as where they had set off from, how they are known to each other and where they were going, it may cast doubt over the credibility of the claim as a whole. It may be that these are simple factual questions that can be addressed by the Claimant's Solicitor at the outset of the claim, and if unsatisfactory responses are forthcoming from the Claimants, it may ring alarm bells that the claim is not a genuine one or requires further scrutiny.

The Role of Accident Management Companies/Claims Companies/Hire Companies

One should be aware of accident management companies, claims companies or hire companies that seek to pursue their own interest in relation to a claim, against that of the Claimant. Claimants' Solicitors should bear in mind that the Claimant is their client and from whom they should take instructions and that instructions should not be taken from the accident management company/claims company or the hire company.

The only purpose of the involvement of the hire company, is to limit the Claimant's liability to the hire company or storage company under the credit hire or storage agreement, as far as practically possible, the hire company/storage company/accident management company should not be the driving force behind the litigation.

The danger of involvement of the credit hire company was highlighted in the case of Farrell and another –v- Direct Accident Management Services Limited and another 2009 EWCA Civ 769. In this case, the hire company, Direct Accident Management Services Limited was ordered to pay 80% of the cost of Birmingham City Council of defending claims brought against it by Mr Farrell and Mr Short. In the index case, the Court found that the credit hire company was liable to pay a third party Costs Order where the terms of the hire agreement and of the Collective Conditional Fee Agreement indicated that it had initiated and controlled litigation brought by the individual to whom it had hired a car.

Another useful case in this respect is *Rasoul & Linkevicius –v- Groupama Insurance Company Limited*, a 2012 decision by Judge Collender QC sitting in the Central London County Court. In this case, the Court made a Wasted Costs Order against the Solicitors where an allegation of fraud was made by the Defendant's insurer and the case collapsed shortly before the Trial. The Court essentially found that the Claimant's Solicitors should have identified the issues earlier in the case and the Judge said:-

> *"Finally to be considered is what happened at Trial. It is recorded by Judge Gerald. The case collapsed in spectacular fashion. Using mild language, the course of the Trial well demonstrated the weakness, if not appropriate nature, of this claim and well supported the assertions made against the claim from an early stage by the Second Defendant. Proper competent work by a Solicitor would have ensured that this case collapsed long before the Trial took place. In my Judgement this is a wholly appropriate case for a Wasted Costs Order to be made against the Claimant's Solicitors".*

It can be said that these cases only go to highlight the importance of proper vetting of cases, prior to accepting them on a Conditional Fee basis by the Claimant Lawyer, and in particular if there is an involvement of an accident management company/claims company or credit hire company sat behind the litigation.

Forensic Engineers – How Useful Are They?

A forensic engineer can be extremely useful in an alleged staged and/or contrived accident. A forensic engineer will be able to look at the damage to both the Claimant's vehicle and the policyholder's vehicle, and form an opinion as whether the damage between the vehicles is consistent or not. This is perhaps a relatively economical investigation, when one considers significant costs that could be spent on a full fraud investigation. The cost of a forensic engineer can be obtained for as little as £500, and will be able to provide an accurate opinion as to whether the damage between the vehicles is consistent with the accident circumstances as reported by the Claimant.

It is not always necessary for the forensic engineer to physically inspect the vehicles involved in the accident, and sometimes a report produced using good quality photographs will be enough. However one should proceed with caution in respect of forensic engineer's reports that have not been produced using good quality photographs or black and white photographs or not showing the full condition of the cars post accident, that were involved in the accident.

Sometimes one sees forensic engineers' reports that have been produced, without all the information concerning the mechanism of the accident, for example, the position of the Claimant's vehicle and the policyholder's vehicle at the moment of impact, the angle of trajectory or the layout of the junction. The angles of the vehicle and whether they were braking etc at the point of impact can often affect the outcome of the forensic engineer's findings as to whether the damage is consistent or not. It is therefore important that before the forensic engineer's report is produced, the forensic engineer has access to the following documents:-

(a) The Claimant's version of events including a sketch plan of the position of the vehicles prior to the accident, the position of the vehicles post accident, and the areas of impact.

(b) The Claimant's Witness Statement confirming the full mechanism of the accident.

(c) Google photographs or a locus plan of where the accident took place.

(d) Clear colour photographs of the damage to both vehicles.

(e) If possible confirmation of the First Defendant's version or policyholder's version of events and sketch plan.

It is clear that the more information the forensic engineer is given, the more likely that his findings or investigations will be accurate.

If the Claimant's Solicitor or the Defendant's insurer has produced and disclosed a forensic engineer's report without all the relevant information, then relevant Part 35 Questions, should be put to the forensic engineer involved, to confirm whether their opinion is altered in relation to the further evidence as outlined above, such as the trajectory of the vehicles at the point of impact, and the layout of the junction. Sometimes cases settle on the basis that all the information has not been obtained before instructing the first engineer's report.

Pre-Action Disclosure Applications

In practice, issuing disclosure Applications can sometimes be very useful under CPR 31.16, prior to the commencement of proceedings, particularly if there is an allegation by the Defendant's insurer that an accident is staged and/or contrived. The Claimant's Solicitor may wish to ask for disclosure of such documents such as CUE searches, MIAFTR searches, photographs of the damage to the respective vehicles, any automotive assessor's report for the Defendant's policyholder's vehicle, a copy of the accident report form, or a copy of the telephone call/transcript reporting the accident.

It may be argued that the accident report form, and/or the initial report of the accident by the policyholder if there is one, cannot be considered a privileged document, unless it was created in contemplation of litigation, and the documents cannot be created in contemplation of litigation, unless the document was created after receipt of the Claims Notification Form and/or Letter of Claim. It may be that prior to the issue of proceedings, Court is only prepared to give disclosure of the automotive assessor's report and photographs for the Defendant's policyholder's vehicle if these are available, but at the very least this should enable the Claimant to obtain an opinion from a forensic engineer, as to whether the damage to the respective vehicles is consistent or not.

Similarly, a Defendant Practitioner, may also wish to obtain the photographs of the damage to the Claimant's vehicle and the automotive assessor's report, for the same reasons.

The Advantages of Part 18 Questions

For the Defendant Lawyer, in alleged staged and/or contrived accidents, Part 18 Questions can be an extremely useful tool in the Defendant's armoury, and are perhaps the most effective tool by which a Defendant insurer can undermine the credibility of the Claimant's case. It is worth a reminder that CPR 18.1 says:-

> *"The Court may at any time order a party to:-*
>
> *(a) "Clarify any matter which is in dispute in the proceedings or give additional information in relation to such matter whether or not the matter is contained or referred to in a Statement of Case".*

There is of course no power for the Court to order that a party responds to a Part 18 Question prior to the commencement of Court proceedings, but it is a useful tactic for the Defendant's insurer to send a set of specific Part 18 Questions to the Claimant's Solicitors, to answer prior to proceedings, and if the questions are not answered before proceedings are issued, the Defendant's insurer can then enforce an Order against the Claimant, after the exchange of Witness Statements.

Of course, Claimant Lawyers in practice will refuse to answer Part 18 Questions prior to the commencement of Court proceedings. Sometimes one sees Claimants that have answered all the Part 18 Questions in a similar manner from a driver and passengers, and/or instances where the Part 18 Questions have been assisted by the accident management company.

When the Claimant's Solicitor deals with the Part 18 Responses, it is prudent to ensure that the Claimant Lawyer ensures that the Part 18 Responses are the answers of the Claimant and no-one else. It is further advisable that as with Witness Statements, the answers to the Part 18 Questions are in the Claimant's own words. In practice, it is advisable for the Claimant's Solicitor to go through the Part 18 Questions with the Claimant, in order to obtain the responses and also assess the relevance of the question.

It may well be that not all of the Part 18 Questions posed by the Defendant's insurer, are relevant to the case and indeed it seems to be the practice of some insurance companies to serve standard sets of Part 18 Questions prior to the commencement of proceedings which appear to be almost identical in every case. The Claimant is only required to answer questions which are proportionate and relevant to the issues in dispute. The Claimant's Solicitors should consider carefully which of the questions are strictly necessary in order to clarify any matters which are in dispute between the parties. Part 18 is not and was never designed to be a fishing expedition for Defendant insurers.

If the Claimant has difficulty with the English language, and/or English is not the Claimant's first language, careful consideration should be given to whether an interpreter is required to complete the Part 18 Request with the Claimant, and sign the appropriate translation certificate. Claimants who cannot read or write English, should not be asked to complete Part 18 Responses in English, and in practice although a legal practitioner can sign a Part 18 Response, where such allegations are being made out by the Defendant, the Claimant should always be given the opportunity to consider the typed responses in detail, and endorse them with a Statement of Truth.

Part 18 Questions can be a very useful tool for Defendant's insurers to undermine the credibility of the Claimant's evidence, provided that such questions are put in a reasonable and proportionate manner.

How Far Should The Investigation Go To Repudiate The Claim?

It is contended that for the Defendant's insurer, staged and/or contrived road traffic accidents are extremely expensive and difficult to investigate. The investigation even for the most basic of claims can run into many tens of thousands of pounds. It is submitted that some of the following investigations, at the outset, may be economical to assist with the repudiation of the claim:-

(a) Obtain copies of the Claimant's medical records. This will enable the Defendant's insurer to confirm any discrepancies between the matters contained within the Claims Notification Forms with regards to medical causation, what is recorded in the medical report, and what is recorded in the General Practitioner or hospital notes. Very often, if a Claimant has not suffered a genuine injury, it is likely that there will be inconsistencies between those three classes of documents.

(b) Part 18 Questions to the Claimants can be an effective investigation, and can seek to further highlight inconsistencies in relation to either factual and/or medical causation and are a particularly useful investigation with regards to previous road traffic accidents.

(c) CUE searches should be undertaken on all of the Claimants to confirm whether they have previous claims or accident history and this should be cross referenced with the medical records and the Part 18 Responses, and the medical report, to confirm whether these have been disclosed.

(d) Checks can be undertaken on the credit hire company and/or the storage company to confirm matters such as VAT registration, insurance on the hire vehicle and the insurance on the Claimant's own vehicle relatively cheaply (please see separate chapter).

(e) An investigator can be instructed to obtain a Statement from the policyholder and enquiries can be made quickly and cheaply with the policyholder by telephone or in writing to confirm the mechanism of the accident and whether it is consistent with the manner in which the Claimant describes the accident occurring.

Perhaps one of the most economical and cheap forms of investigation is a forensic engineer's report who can tell whether the damage between the vehicles is consistent or not with the accident circumstances as described by the Claimant and the policyholder. Often inconsistent vehicle damage between the two vehicles will lead to a much more detailed investigation by the Defendant's insurer in relation to the mechanism of the accident and the claims presented.

The difficulty for Defendant's insurers and Defendant Lawyers is often the Claimant's Solicitors will be reluctant to answer detailed sets of Part 18 Questions prior to the commencement of proceedings, and the Claimant's Solicitors will often be reluctant to disclose medical records and/or large volumes of documents before proceedings commence.

In a similar way, the Defendant's insurer will often be reluctant to disclose the full nature of its investigations until the Claimant has confirmed the responses to the Part 18 Questions. This reluctance by both sides to share information and/or documents can sometimes cause proceedings to be commenced unnecessarily by the Claimant Lawyers and then discontinue quickly once the Defence is received confirming the nature of the Defendant's insurer's investigations.

From a Defendant's perspective, it may be argued that the appropriate time to disclose the nature of the investigations to the Claimant's Solicitors together with the appropriate documentation is upon receipt of the responses to the Part 18 Questions, endorsed with statement of truth and/or in indemnity cases, ie allegations of phantom passengers, slam on induced accidents, or no collision allegations, as soon as a Statement and signed proof of evidence has been taken from the Defendant's policyholder to confirm the nature of the allegations being put by the Defendant's insured. It can be argued that once the

Defendant knows what the allegations are, there is no benefit to either party in withholding the information.

Currently talks are ongoing between the Claimant bodies of APIL and MASS (The Association of Personal Injury Lawyers and the Motor Accident Solicitors Society) and the Defendant representative bodies including The Association of British Insurers (ABI) to try and encourage the sharing of data between Claimants' Solicitors and Defendants' insurers, long before proceedings are ever issued. It is contended that this can only be in everyone's best interests including Defendants' insurers and Claimants' Solicitors, to seek to share data and eradicate fraudulent claims at the outset. The outcome of these discussions remains to be seen.

Indemnity & The 2002 European Communities Regulations

The 2002 European Communities (Rights Against Insurers) Regulations 2002 state:

> *"Regulation 3 – Right of Action.*
>
> *Paragraph 1 of this Regulation applies where an entitled party is a cause of action against an insured person in tort or (as the case may be) delict, and that cause of action arises out of an accident.*
>
> *Paragraph 2 where this paragraph applies, the entitled party may, without prejudice to his right to issue proceedings against the insured person, issue proceedings against the insurer who issued the policy of insurance relating to the insured vehicle, and that insurer shall be directly liable to the entitled party to the extent that he is liable to the insured person".*

This means, in the ordinary course of events, that the Claimant can recover compensation directly from the insurance company rather than pursuing the policyholder responsible.

The difficulty that arises in road traffic accident, allegation or fraud cases, is often the road traffic accident insurer will refuse or reserve indemnity to the First Defendant, being the policyholder pending the outcome of investigations. The question is then whether the Claimant can still pursue a cause of action under the 2002 Regulations.

It is usually prudent for the Claimant to issue proceedings against both the insurer and the Defendant driver directly, given that there will always almost be a valid cause of action, against the driver of the vehicle and/or the Defendant's servant and/or agent if the vehicle was being driven on behalf of an employer, the Defendant's insurer will usually be liable to satisfy any unsatisfied Judgment under the relevant provisions of the Road Traffic Act 1988. However, if indemnity has been reserved by the insurer and not refused, there is an argument that the insurer will still be liable under the provisions of the 2002 European Communities Rights Against Insurers Regulations, if indemnity has not been correctly withdrawn under the policy. The wording of paragraph 2 of Regulation 3 which deals with this is whether the insurer is *"liable to the insured person"*. There is an argument that the insurer will be *"liable to the insured person"* in the circumstances that indemnity has not been withdrawn in accordance with the relevant terms and conditions of the policy of insurance. If indemnity has been reserved, then the Claimant may wish to ask the following questions/documents perhaps by way of Part 18 / 31.12 request of the Defendant's insurance company:-

(a) Why has indemnity been reserved?

(b) A copy of the policy of insurance and the Certificate of Insurance.

(c) A copy of the terms and conditions of the policy.

It is arguable that these documents should be disclosed in order that the Claimant can make the relevant enquiries to check whether it still has a cause of action under the 2002 Regulations. In reality, most insurance companies will want the Claimant to have a Judgment if anything, under the 1988 Road Traffic Act, as opposed to the 2002 Regulations, given that if an insurer has to satisfy a Judgment under the 1988 Act, it will allow the insurer to pursue the policyholder for the Judgment costs and damages, in the event that the event that indemnity has been correctly refused.

The Claimant Lawyer will of course argue that they have no idea why indemnity has been refused to the First Defendant, and it will be up to the Defendant's insurer, usually the Second Defendant in the proceedings, to prove why indemnity has been withdrawn from the policyholder and it has been withdrawn correctly in accordance with the terms and conditions of the policy.

If indemnity has been refused, then the Claimant will also arguably require the Defendant's insurer to prove this. In such circumstances, the Claimant may ask for disclosure of the policy of insurance, the policy schedule, the letter refusing indemnity and the terms and conditions of the policy to prove that indemnity has been withdrawn in accordance with the terms and conditions of the policy. If indemnity has not been withdrawn correctly, the Claimant may wish to argue that he still has a direct cause of action under the 2002 Regulations. It is clear however that to protect the cause of action the Defendant's driver should always be added to the proceedings as an additional party to protect the cause of action under the 1988 Road Traffic Act.

When Should Indemnity Be Reserved/Refused?

It can be argued, that the answer to this question is that indemnity should be reserved or refused to the policyholder, in the circumstances where the Defendant's insurer has enough information from investigations, which show a prima facie case of fraud. An insurance contract is a contract of utmost good faith, and if there is cogent evidence to suggest that the policyholder has mis-declared the facts to his insurance company either about the circumstances of the accident in question, his claims history, information used upon which the insurance company has underwritten the policy then this should be enough to refuse indemnity by the insurer.

However the insurer's letter refusing indemnity to the policyholder must make it clear to the policyholder upon what basis the insurance cover has been withdrawn and on what basis cover has been withdrawn with reference to the relevant terms and conditions of the policy. Sometimes, it becomes evident from letters withdrawing indemnity, that the insurer has not really considered upon what basis indemnity has been withdrawn and it has simply been withdrawn due to "concerns" about the claim. It is arguable that this is not enough to withdraw indemnity under the policy, and the reasons for the withdrawal of indemnity must make it clear why the insurance company considers that the contract of insurance has been breached and potentially should disclose any evidence in support of the breach, to avoid a claim by the policyholder for a contribution and/or indemnity if the Claimant subsequently issues proceedings against both the driver and the insurer for a contribution and/or indemnity under the policy of insurance.

Further comments in relation to contracts of insurance are outside the scope of this book, but indemnity arguments are a useful tool in the Claimant's Lawyer's armoury, if considering a cause of action under the 2002 Regulations, if allegations of fraud have been made by the Defendant's insurer and indemnity has been reserved or refused.

A final point is that if indemnity has been "reserved" in the Defence, then it is arguable that the documentation such as the insurance certificate and schedule of insurance becomes a disclosable document, given that the Claimant's Solicitor needs to know whether the 2002 Regulations still apply and in particular whether the Defendant's insurer is "liable to the insured person, under the 2002 Regulations". It should also be borne in mind, that if the Defendant's insurer wishes to refuse indemnity and withdraws the policy it has a number of statutory mechanisms in order to do this. This is relevant in that that Defendant's policyholder may have sought declaration proceedings under Section 152(2) of the Road Traffic Act 1988.

Making Investigations Into The Policyholder

If the Defendant's insurer considers that a claim is potentially fraudulent, and/or there are concerns about the claim, the following investigations may be made into the policyholder:-

(a) Confirmation that the policyholder resides at the home address which may involve a visit from an insurance investigator to confirm the identity of the policyholder and the accident circumstances. The Defendant's insurer should be careful to ensure that if the Claimant's first language is not English that any letters or correspondence and/or telephone calls are made and/or written in the policyholder's own language.

(b) Investigations can be made via address searches databases such as Experian to confirm if the policyholder has ever lived at the address on the policy, and/or has any claims links to other addresses on other policies of insurance and/or claims.

(c) Investigations can be made into the policyholder's claims history and whether the policyholder has been involved in any previous or similar road traffic collisions involving similar circumstances and checks should be made to ensure that these have been reported to the insurer on cover.

(d) If the policyholder has disappeared, enquiries can be made with the policyholder's friends, family or at previous addresses to confirm the identity of the policyholder and/or if there is a genuine reason why the policyholder is not responding to correspondence and/or letters.

(e) Investigations can be made in relation to any other claims that the policyholder has made on previous policies or claims via the claims underwriting database, in order to confirm whether there were any "concerns" in relation to the policyholder's previous claims or accidents, and Section 29(3) Data Protection Act requests can be made to the relevant insurers of the information.

It is clear that in terms of an economic and efficient investigation, the policyholder should be the Defendant's insurer's first port of call in relation to concerns about a road traffic accident and whether the Defendant's own policyholder can withstand the scrutiny of the investigation.

In a similar way, the Claimant's Lawyer, if the Defendant's insurer is raising concerns about the policyholder and refusing indemnity, it is prudent for the Claimant's Solicitor to undertake enquiries with the Defendant's policyholder to try and trace the policyholder in the event that the Defendant's insurer says that he cannot be traced. There is nothing in principle, preventing the Claimant's insurer interviewing the Defendant's policyholder, provided that the Defendant's policyholder is not represented by Solicitors, and his advice to seek independent legal advice, prior to the interview taking place.

Recovery Against Proved Fraudulent Claimants

The unfortunate reality of allegations of fraud cases is that even where the Defendant's insurer succeeds in making out the allegations at Trial, ie that an accident is staged or contrived, it is often very difficult for the Defendant's insurer to recover costs against the Claimant and/or the after the event insurer. Normally, the after the event insurance policy will have a clause in it which sets out that if the Claimant refuses to co-operate with his Solicitors, the prospects of success are less than 50%, a finding of fraud or exaggeration is made at Trial by the Judge, then the after the event insurer is unlikely to indemnify the Defendant's costs in such circumstances.

In a similar way, often the fraudulent Claimant will move his assets into the names of other persons and will have little if anything of material value in his name in order that the Defendant's insurance company can recover their costs. In those circumstances, where the Defendant's insurer has managed to obtain a Costs Order against the Claimant directly, the following matters may be of assistance in order to investigate recovering the costs against the Claimant directly:-

(a) Financial searches through Experian can be undertaken on the Claimant's assets including any property or vehicles owned, any monies stashed away in bank accounts, in order to consider Charging Orders on the property, a third party Order for monies that are sitting in the Claimant's account, or an attachment of earnings order, if it can be established that the Claimant is in gainful employment. The most common type of Order and the most efficient Order is often a Charging Order against the property.

(b) In very rare cases, if during the course of the litigation, it can be established that the Claimant is seeking to avoid an address for service, or frequently changes the address for service, then the Defendant's insurer could consider security for costs Order, but again the mechanics of this are outside the scope of this book.

If the Defendant's insurer has suspicions that either the hire company, Solicitors or an accident management company are either funding the litigation or have control of the litigation the Defendant's insurer could consider a third party Costs Order against the party as occurred in Farrell and another –v- Direct Accident Management Services Limited 2008. The jurisdiction to make such an Order arises under Section 51 of the Senior Courts Act but this gives no guidance on when such a third party Costs Order should be made and the sub-section provides:-

> That Costs Orders are in the discretion of the Court and in sub-section 3 "*the Court shall have full power to determine by whom and to what extent the costs are to be paid*".

In *Symphony Group plc –v- Hodgson 1994 QB179* Lord Justice Balcombe stated that an Order for payment of costs by a non party will always be "exceptional". In *Dymocks Franchise Systems NSWPTY Limited –v- Todd 2004 UKPC 39* Lord Brown clarified "*exceptional in this context means no more than outside the ordinary run of cases where parties defend claims for their own benefit and at their own expense. The ultimate question of any such exceptional case is whether in all the circumstances it is just to make an Order*".

It can be argued that the reality therefore it seems is that the Court is unlikely to make such an Order unless it can be shown that the hire company, accident management company or Solicitors had control or funding of the litigation in some way and there will have to be cogent evidence of this. Part 18 Questions and/or an Application for specific disclosure may be a useful tool in such circumstances.

Alleged Staged/Contrived Accidents – A Warning

In a recent case His Honour Judge Mitchell sitting in Central London in the case of Ostrach –v- McGreal and Others 2013 dismissing eight alleged link staged accidents stated:

> *"it is manifest that dishonesty was rife --- I hope that this message going out from this Court will be that if people lend their names to this kind of swindle they risk going to prison.... I hope that some publicity can be given to this case so that members of the public can be made aware of the consequences of members of the public getting involved, namely prison"*

And he then went on to give a warning to Solicitors:-

> *"They should think long and hard when there are no witnesses being called to corroborate the accident. This may be a pointer to the fact that the accident is staged and in my Judgment it could be an abuse of process to proceed with such claims".*

It is clear that a number of Courts including London, Birmingham, Manchester and Cardiff who deal with lots of these types of cases, are now prepared to take a robust approach to this type of alleged fraud. It is therefore essential that the Solicitors know their client and have met with the clients in Conference prior to the Trial, and/or had a robust Conference with Counsel prior to the matters proceeding to Trial. It is clear from the general tone of Circuit Judges sitting in these Courts, that they are not prepared to tolerate this type of fraud and will have no hesitation in the referral of Claimants to the CPS and/or proceedings for contempt of Court of their own motion for Claimants who engage in this type of activity.

CHAPTER THREE
FRAUD RINGS: HOW TO IDENTIFY AND INVESTIGATE

How To Identify If The Case Is Being Investigated As Part Of A Fraud Ring

A fraud ring may be broadly defined as a group of one or more road traffic accidents which share a common dominator as part of the alleged fraud, and it may be the accident management company, the hire company, the storage company, the Claimant, a group of addresses. The Defendant's insurer, will seek to investigate, a group of accidents together which have similar evident circumstances, and the links may be through one or more of the above denominators.

The last few years, this type of fraud has become more prolific and now within Defendant Solicitors and insurers, there are dedicated teams of claims handlers and Lawyers dealing with such claims. The insurers' internal systems will often be geared towards spotting the signs of a fraud ring, and then it is often the case that more cases are brought into the fraud ring investigation, as the indicators become clearer. More often than not, a fraud ring will involve the same type of fraud, i.e. there may be a group of accidents which have all the hallmarks of a staged or contrived accident, and/or they may be a group of accidents linked through slam on or induced accident scenario. More often than not, when a fraud ring is being investigated, it will often be the same group of individuals that are instigating the fraud but not always. If you are a Claimant Lawyer, it may well be that you have a number of cases from a specific hire company or accident management company or a particular referral source and you have been targeted as part of a fraud ring to progress the claims, it could be that the hire company or accident management company, has passed the claim to a number of different Solicitors in order to avoid the fraud being identified.

This chapter is intended predominantly for Claimant Lawyers, to advise Claimant Lawyers how they can spot the warning signs in relation to fraud rings, and implement systems within practice to try and avoid them.

Spotting The Warning Signs – Hire Companies and Accident Management Companies

If Solicitors are dealing with personal injury work, and in particular work from hire companies and accident management companies and/or referral sources, it is key to know the identity of the work, where it is coming from and the referral source of the work. This is still the case even though referral fees are now banned.

It is arguable, that Claimant Lawyers should have systems and processes in place to identify and prevent fraud rings, particularly if that law firm has been targeted in the past by unscrupulous accident management companies or other referral sources of work. It would be wise that if all the work is coming from one referral source hire company, storage company or accident management company, then it may be prudent to have one fee earner or a group of fee earners dealing with those cases as it allows the fee earners to spot trends or patterns in cases quickly and easily as compared to firms which allocate that work to different fee earners, across the firm.

In the alternative, it may be prudent to have a system in place, where the Case Management system can spot trends in cases electronically and concerns may be raised by some more of the following factors it is submitted:-

(a) A significant number of accidents in a firm's caseload which occurs at one specific location.

(b) A large grouping of claims from the same person or group of individuals within a short space of time.

(c) A large number of concerns raised by an insurance company to a specific group or grouping of claims that are coming from the same referral source hire company or accident management company.

(d) A referral source or client who suddenly wants to refer large volumes of cases to a particular firm without good reason.

(e) A large group of claims coming from similar addresses or a particular area without any clear explanation for the source of the work.

(f) A large volume of road traffic accidents being referred to the Claimant Lawyer within a short period of time, from one source.

(g) A significant number of accidents, that are occurring with similar individuals in similar circumstances any real explanation.

It is of course the case, that the Claimant's Solicitor has a duty of confidentiality to the client, if suspicions are raised on each individual case. Claimants' Solicitors should be alive to the fact it is argued, that such fraud rings are more common than one would perhaps think, and putting a system or process in place to identify potentially fraudulent claims and provide scrutiny over those claims is key especially when the Claimant's Solicitor is conducting the litigation on a Conditional Fee basis.

How The Insurers Investigate Fraud Rings And The Types Of Databases

There are a number of tools open to insurers in order to investigate potential fraud rings and these may be broadly summarised as follows:-

(a) Computer databases such as Experian, allow insurers to undertake address searches to link potential claims that have been submitted via different addresses which share the same or similar accident circumstances or individuals involved in those claims which may be the policyholder or the Claimants involved in the accident, or this may equally involve the hire company, accident management company or numerous other individuals.

(b) Insurers have sophisticated fraud detection systems which means that often a computer system may flag that an accident has occurred in similar circumstances, with similar individuals and flag this up to the claims handler as being part of a wider group of claims which can trigger a wider investigation.

(c) Investigations can be made into the accident management company or hire company or referral source behind the claim, to establish the manner in which claims are being submitted with potential links to other claims.

(d) CUE Underwriting Exchange, allows insurers to establish other claims made from various individual Claimants or policyholders, to confirm if previous claims have been made in similar circumstances or with similar factual circumstances or with similar groups of individuals.

(e) The MIAFTR database, will identify if vehicles have been subject to previous total losses or have sustained previous damage which has led to a write off of the vehicle. This information is recorded on MIAFTR by the insurers, and if that vehicle is then involved in a subsequent claim, the insurers can check whether those vehicles, have been involved in previous claims with similar circumstances.

(f) Finally, most of the large Defendant Solicitors, have their own internal databases for the investigation of fraud ring claims for claims linked to potential fraud rings, and data searches can be undertaken internally, in order to confirm whether individuals, vehicles, accident management companies etc have any links to other claims that are being investigated as part of the potential fraud ring.

It should be borne in mind that a fraud ring could be anything from ten claims or so all the way up to hundreds of potential claims by similar individuals submitted in similar circumstances. There are a number of publicised cases where individuals have been sent to prison for cases involving fraud rings. The Claimant Lawyer will not have the benefit of the above data searches, in order to identify potentially fraudulent claims or claims that form part of a fraud ring, but the Claimant Lawyer can request access and copies of the searches from the Defendant's insurers. It is therefore essential, that Claimant law firms are aware of the potential risks arising out of fraud rings, and have systems in place to spot them internally and to deal with them if they should so arise.

Linking Potential Parties, Facebook, Data Mining and Vehicles

As fraud detection systems become ever more sophisticated, and indeed it may be argued that as the fraudsters themselves become ever more sophisticated to detection techniques, thorough methods of detection and identification of potentially fraudulent claims have emerged.

Facebook and in particular friends on Facebook, have become popular methods of detection for Defendant insurers in the fight against potentially fraudulent claims. It may be argued that Facebook is an extremely useful tool for Defendant insurers and Solicitors when attempting to establish links between the driver and passengers of the policyholder's vehicle and alleged driver and passengers of the Claimant's vehicle. However, one must be careful to ensure that the alleged Facebook links are relevant to the case in question. One sometimes sees hundreds of pages of disclosure by Defendant insurers in relation to alleged Facebook links much of them with little relevance to the Claimants in question to the case. It is therefore essential that any links that are pleaded in the Defence concerning Facebook or other social media sites, are linked to the Claimants in question.

Defendants' insurers should also be careful to ensure that any alleged links are actually the person that is specified in the pleading. There are many individuals on Facebook and other social media sites with the same Christian name and surname. Some may even share the same date of birth. It is therefore essential that if allegations are being made on the basis of Facebook links or other links via social media, further checks via Experian and other verification processes need to ensure that the links are through the people that are being alleged. Before the Defendant insurer discloses any links, it is prudent to have the

Claimants verify a Statement of Truth on Part 18 Responses, in order to confirm whether they know the alleged individuals, and if so when, how and in what capacity the persons are known. A denial of a link, will have little evidential value unless it has been endorsed with a Statement of Truth.

From a Claimant perspective, Claimant Lawyers will want to ensure, that Claimants are carefully questioned about any alleged Facebook links or other social media links to the persons in the other car, and in particular to go through any address details or alleged linked addresses that are pleaded in the Defence. There may be other links pleaded to vehicles, other claims or addresses. It is important to a Reply to the Defence, that the Claimant addresses all of the alleged links and confirms the link or denies it appropriately and if the link is known specify how the link has emerged. One sometimes finds that there are credible explanations for links through Facebook and the like which may lead to settlement of the case if explained.

If a Defendant insurer wishes to adduce Facebook links or other data searches from CUE, then it is important that the Defendant insurer drafts a detailed Witness Statement usually from the claims handler at the insurance company with conduct of the case, explaining how the searches have been conducted, what search terms were used, in what capacity the searches were conducted, why they were conducted and the findings as a result of those searches. It is prudent if the person who has conducted the actual search also provides a Statement. Facebook searches and other database searches, are of little evidential value without a Statement in support of the searches. The Statement will usually require a lot of explanation in order to explain the alleged links and how those links have been discovered through data mining.

Tackling Fraud Rings, Collapsing Them Like A Pack Of Cards

It may be argued that one of the most effective ways for Defendant insurers in dealing with fraud rings or alleged fraud rings, is tackling the individuals at the centre of the fraud ring and the centre of the fraud. This may be the credit hire company, storage company or accident management company, and individuals can be dealt with, it may well be that the rest of these fall away. It may be argued that one of the difficulties in dealing with fraud ring cases is knowing where to start with the investigation, and what is most likely to be the most efficient methods of investigation.

One of the most effective investigations is instructing insurance investigators to visit the credit hire company, accident management company or the individuals who are believed to be at the centre of the fraud, in order to obtain Witness Statements. Undoubtedly, data searches including Facebook, CUE and other insurance databases, are always going to be the key to tackling this type of fraud. In order to understand the potential fraud, one needs to set out the entire map and the links between the cases, in order to understand who is at the centre of the scam whether it has been orchestrated by those involved, in order to effectively tackle it. The unfortunate situation is that all of this costs a huge amount of money for insurance companies in undertaking such investigations. When dealing with litigation of such cases, the Defendant's insurer may always want to make an early Application in such cases to consolidate any cases that are ongoing into one set of claims that can be case managed together. The Court trying all of the cases together, allows the same Trial Judge to hear the separate road traffic accidents consecutively in order to draw conclusions in relation to a series of cases as opposed to them being heard by individual Judges on an individual basis. Claimant Lawyers, will of course wish to resist any such Application.

Tactically, the difficulty for Claimant Lawyers in some circumstances is that if a potentially credible case is heard with a number of other alleged fraudulent road traffic claims, there is a risk that the "good case" will be tainted by the other poorer Claimants in the other alleged cases. It may therefore be prudent, for the Claimant to resist any Application to consolidate a claim, unless there is a confirmed link with the other people, parties or vehicles in the other cases. In CPR 3, the Court has the power to make an Order that cases be managed together with one set of Court proceedings. This is common sense in a case where there are driver and a number of passengers in the same road traffic accident, and it is clear that these should always be heard in the same set of Court proceedings.

However what is less clear is if the Defendant's insurer alleges that the Claimant's case is linked to other separate road traffic collisions without any direct links to the Claimant. One sometimes sees Defences drafted where there are alleged links between road traffic accidents but pleaded in relation to address matches obtained from Experian for other alleged accidents or claims which have emanated from the same address. In the alternative the alleged link to another road traffic accident, may be that the parties utilise the same credit hire or storage company which is alleged to have been the subject to other alleged fraudulent road traffic claims. The Claimant Lawyer may want to resist such an Application to consolidate with the other road traffic accidents, unless the Defendant's insurer can show a solid link between the road traffic collisions by way of people, places or vehicles i.e. there is a link between the Claimant and his passengers and/or the policyholder and passengers which is denied in a Facebook entry or evidence such as the Claimant and policyholder have the same address in the past and the link is denied etc. The Courts tend not to consolidate cases with other road traffic accidents, unless a direct link can be shown and the link between the road traffic accident is a relevant one.

It therefore follows, that if the Defendant's insurer is making an Application to consolidate alleged linked road traffic claims, the Application must set in detail the nature of the alleged links, and provide evidence in support. It is arguable that vague pleadings in the Defence about previous claims at addresses that the Claimant has never visited, utilising an accident management company which has been subject to another claim, without any direct links to the accident in question, can be argued is unlikely to be enough to consolidate the claims and the Court proceedings or case manage them consecutively. The Application must have evidence in support.

When Is A Claimant Sometimes An Innocent Victim?

In practice, there may be occasions when the Claimant is alleged to have formed part of a fraud ring, when they have been caught up in a potentially fraudulent road traffic claim orchestrated by other individuals, but have actually not been involved in the fraud themselves. An example may be, a vehicle which is struck in the rear by a multiple occupancy vehicle at a set of traffic lights. The Claimants and passengers in the vehicle have a genuine reason for the journey and allege that the policyholder's vehicle has been driven into the back of them at a speed of approximately 30 miles an hour, and the Claimants suggest that there was unusual behaviour from the passengers of the policyholder's vehicle after the accident, for example they say that following the accident the passengers in the policyholder's vehicle, get out of the vehicle holding their necks in a theatrical fashion and complaining of whiplash type injuries.

The Claimants themselves in the vehicle that has been struck sustain minor whiplash injuries and wish to make a claim for vehicle damage. Sometimes when one questions the Claimant, it may emerge that in fact the vehicle has driven into them on purpose for the purpose of making fraudulent road traffic claims for the passengers of the vehicle which has struck them. It is alleged that the Claimants are involved in the alleged fraud in some way in the vehicle that has been struck, one should be careful to question the Claimant to clarify with them whether there was anything odd about the accident or the behaviour from passengers of the vehicle which struck them. It is a sad fact and it seems that road traffic accidents frauds have now become so prevalent, that innocent members of the public are becoming victims of such scams, and in some circumstances the Defendant's insurers are then making allegations for fraud against the people who have been innocent victims of a road traffic accident. It has to be said that it is sometimes difficult to separate out the genuine Claimants in such an accident, as to the ones that have actually been involved in orchestrating the fraud. However, if it is alleged that the Claimants have formed part of a fraud ring or have been involved in some kind of staged or contrived collision, the Claimant Lawyers should always investigate the circumstances and mechanism of the accident, and in particular the behaviour of the passengers from the vehicle which strikes the Claimant's vehicle, if it seems from the interview that the Claimants are telling the truth about the circumstances of the accident, but something does not seem quite right about it from the claims presented from the other vehicle. One should be alive potentially to the possibility that the Claimants are the innocent victims in a potential scam. This occurrence is relatively rare in practice but one that should always be considered if something does not seem entirely correct about the claims from the other vehicle i.e. they have been withdrawn without notice as soon as the allegation is raised by the Defendant's insurer.

CHAPTER FOUR
SLAM ONS / INDUCED ACCIDENTS

Spotting The Warning Signs

There are a number of potential warning signs of a staged/induced accident. A staged/induced accident may be broadly defined as a vehicle which slams on its brakes for no reason in order to induce an accident. A common scenario may be a vehicle which is setting off from a roundabout, and it braked for no reason as it enters the roundabout causing the vehicle behind to go into the back of it so the occupants of the vehicle braking can make claims for compensation. Another type of alleged fraud is a decoy vehicle type accident where two vehicles work in conjunction with each other and the vehicle in front brakes for no given reason and this may be at the exit to a junction from an A road or a turn into a side road, the vehicle behind it being driven by the vigilant person also brakes and causes the vehicle behind it i.e. the innocent motorist to go into the back of the middle vehicle and the vehicle which caused that vehicle to brake disappears never to be seen again.

One or more of the following factors may be indicative that the claim needs to be investigated as a slam on induced/contrived accident.

Very often, the criminal gangs engaged in this type of activity will target commercial vehicles i.e. white van men because they assume that such individuals will either not report the accident to their employer, or will not engage in the process of challenging the claims.

It is also a sad fact, that some fraudsters target elderly people or single mothers and other individuals in society who the fraudsters think may not necessarily challenge a claim. The difficulty for the fraudsters is that this type of fraud has become more prevalent and due to the publicity of these types of cases in the media, the general public have become more aware of groups of cases. This was highlighted in the case of Baljinder Gill who was killed when her car was hit by a van on the A40 in Buckinghamshire.

Some other common features of this type of fraud may be as follows:-

(a) The Claimants do not have a clear reason for the journey they are making.

(b) Multiple occupancy vehicles and a large number of personal injury claims from both vehicles.

(c) Similar whiplash injuries emanating from all of the vehicles which do not appear to be supported by medical records.

(d) Odd behaviour of Claimants following the accident such as laughing or joking or holding their necks in a theatrical fashion.

(e) Claims history of the Claimants involved in the accident and significant numbers of road traffic accidents in a short period of time.

(f) The policyholder suggesting that the vehicles in front were being driven in conjunction with each other prior to the accident.

(g) Unlikely reasons for braking such as animals running out into the road, and other reasons which seem far fetched.

Investigating Claims and Challenging Credibility

It is arguable, that the key to the success or failure of a case where the Defendant's insurer has raised that it was a slam on or induced accident is going to be arguably the credibility of the Claimant and therefore as soon as the allegation is raised by the Defendant's insurer, it may be prudent to ask a number of questions by the Claimant for the Claimant Lawyer to assess the credibility of the client and some of the questions may be as follows:-

(a) Was there a genuine reason for braking, and if so what was it?

(b) If it was another vehicle that caused the Claimant's vehicle to brake, were the people in the vehicle in front known to the Claimant and if so, how?

(c) What was the reason for the journey?

(d) Where had the Claimant set off from, and where were they going to?

(e) How were the Claimants in the vehicle known to each other?

(f) How long had they known each other and where did they meet?

(g) The driver and the passengers should be interviewed separately, to ensure that the mechanisms of the accident are consistent between the driver and the passengers.

It is arguable that one should particularly look out for far fetched or potentially unrealistic reasons for the Claimant's journey at the time of the accident. A common theme in some of these cases is sometimes that the Claimants were going to look at a vehicle at the time of the accident they had seen in the Autotrader or other car advertisement magazines. Sometimes the Claimant may be asked the question who they were going to meet and they are reluctant to give an answer or reply "a friend". In such circumstances, the Claimant should be pressed for specifics as to who they were going to meet, where they were going to meet them and what was the purpose of the meeting. For example if the Claimants say that they had been shopping at a well known supermarket, is there a receipt for the shopping or the items purchased or bank statements or the like? If the Claimants say that they were going to purchase a vehicle or view a vehicle, is there a copy of the vehicle advertisement, and can a copy of this be obtained from the relevant subscription?

It is key that there is some evidence to support the reason for the journey and the Claimants all being in the accident location at the time when it occurs and if there is not, it may lead one to question the credibility of the claim as a whole.

One may also wish to investigate whether the reason for the Claimant's journey makes practical sense. With the advent of modern technology such as Google maps, one can plot the journey from the set off point to the intended destination to see if the Claimant's journey makes sense for where they were going. At the outset of the case all the Claimants should be asked to produce a sketch plan and a map to show the intended route. They should also be asked to show a sketch plan of the accident circumstances including the position of the vehicles pre and post accident and the impact points of damage and the documents between the driver and the passengers should be compared for consistency.

It is arguable, that some or more of the following indicators, may lead one to question whether there is something not quite right about the claim:-

(a) The driver or the passengers in the vehicle refusing to co-operate or answer questions about the accident, particularly if themselves are pursuing claims.

(b) As soon as the allegation of fraud is raised by the insurer or con cerns are raised by the insurer, the driver or passenger in the vehicle, suddenly deciding they no longer wish to pursue the claim. One should take into account that such an allegation is always going to make any genuine Claimants nervous, but most genuine Claimants still wish to pursue their claims even at this point and it may lead one to question why such a Claimant no longer wishes to pursue a claim when the allegation is raised.

(c) A number of the Claimants disappearing or becoming uncooperative.

(d) The Claimant refusing to answer the telephone calls or engage in a Conference with Counsel about the claim and to correspond in writing only or via an accident management or hire company. It is accepted that this may be explained if there are language difficulties and the like.

(e) As in other chapters, it may be prudent that where such allegations are raised by the Defendant's insurer that the Claimants are invited into the office for interview or at the very least a detailed telephone conversation/Conference takes place with all of the Claimants about the allegations, to establish whether there is a consistent and credible version of events and at the very least a credible reason for having brought the vehicle to a stop. It is arguable, that one should be very wary about claims involving commercial vehicles running into the back of a Claimant's vehicle where there is a decoy vehicle in front, and this type of fraud now seems to be more prevalent than ever before.

It is arguable, that there are a number of effective methods for challenging the credibility of these cases such as Part 18s, and data searches discussed elsewhere in other chapters, but arguably the most effective method of defeating these cases and where arguably they tend to fail at Trial is not on the accident circumstances themselves, as these tend often to be well rehearsed but they can sometimes be defeated simply in relation to causation arguments over injury and this is discussed further.

How Cases Can Be Defeated Using Causation Arguments

It may be argued that one of the ways in which a Defendant Lawyer can defeat the Claimant's case is with the use of causation arguments. If the Claimant has not suffered a genuine injury, then both the Claimant and the Defendant's Lawyer may find that the claim has significant inconsistencies, in relation to the claim for general damages. In such circumstances, the following investigations may be useful in relation to the causation arguments which undermine the Claimant's credibility:-

(a) Look at the Claimant's CNF form, which is of course a document that has been verified by a Statement of Truth. What injuries are recorded in the CNF form, what is said about the time away from work in the CNF form and when medical treatment was first sought and where.

(b) Compare this to the consistency of the reporting of the injuries, loss of earnings and GP or hospital attendance in the medical report. Is the Claimant consistent in the medical report about these matters and further when he first experienced pain in the areas affected and how long the pain in each particular injury lasted for, together with the effect on home, work and social life, and in particular any sporting activities.

(c) Compare this for consistency with the Claimant's medical records and in particular the areas of the body affected by the injury, mechanism of the accident, any attendances there were at the General Practitioners, and if the Claimant was reporting about the severity of his symptoms. One should also look to the medical report to confirm whether the Claimant advised the expert about any previous accidents or pain or suffering in the areas affected by the injuries.

(d) Compare this for consistency with the Witness Statement and/or Part 18 Responses, in order to confirm whether the Claimant was consistent here concerning the above matters and in particular how long the injuries took to recover, the effect on home, work and social life, attendances at the GP/hospital, accident history and previous history of whiplash injuries or neck or back pain.

It may be argued that it is often the case, that where the Claimant has not suffered a genuine injury, that there will be inconsistencies between these documents, and for the Defendant Lawyer it is always worth putting a set of Part 18 Questions to the Claimant, on this basis.

When undertaking a Conference or the interview going through the Defendant's allegations, it is essential that the Claimant Lawyer asks these questions of the Claimant. There is little point in attempting to win a Trial on the issues of liability, if a claim on causation is going to fail.

Burden Of Proof In Relation To Alleged Induced Accident Claims

It should be borne in mind, that it is up to the Claimant to prove on the balance of probability that there was a genuine reason for the Claimant to brake, which was the cause of the accident. However, if the Defendant's insurer pleads fraud in such a case, then it will be up to the Defendant's insurance company to prove that the Claimant braked for no particular reason, causing the collision on purpose. This is in the same way that if the Defendant's insurer pleads fraud in relation to decoy vehicle type accidents, then it will be up to the Defendant's insurer also to prove the claim was fraudulent in the same way.

How Can They Be Investigated?

The Claimant's first contemporaneous reporting of the accident circumstances will usually be the hospital or General Practitioner records. It is always worth checking the medical records or hospital records to see whether this is consistent with the Claimant's instructions about the way in which the accident occurred.

The medical report should be also checked to ensure that the accident circumstances reported to the medical expert are consistent with the ones recorded during the Claimant's initial interview. You should bear in mind, that medical experts do not always record accident circumstances correctly, and particularly if there is a language barrier and there was no translator present for the medical examination. If any inconsistency arises as a result of a medical examination particularly in relation to the accident circumstances, one may ensure that original copies of the notes from the examination are obtained from the medical practitioner.

In the era of fixed costs, it is now even more important that detailed instructions are taken at the Claims Notification stage of the case, and at the outset as to the circumstances of the accident. One should ensure that these details are correctly recorded in the Claims Notification form and this is checked by the Claimant before it is submitted to the Defendant's insurer, given that the document contains a Statement of

Truth. Sometimes one sees the accident circumstances recorded in such a document as a simple rear end collision whereas the Claimant's instructions were in fact that the vehicle in front caused him to brake and where these details are missing from the Claims Notification Form or the Letter of Claim this can be damaging to the Claimant's credibility at a later stage when the Claimant is cross examined as to why these details only materialised at a later stage when the Defendant puts the allegation that it was a slam on type accident.

It is always prudent to ensure that where the Claimant's credibility is going to be key to the success or failure of the case and where the Defendant's insurer makes the allegation pre issue it will be extremely important to take detailed Witness Statements from the Claimant and any of his passengers before proceedings are issued to check the consistency of the evidence between the parties and especially in relation to the reasons as to why each of the Claimants say that they had to brake. Be aware especially of witnesses who give exactly the same version of events without any discrepancy which may suggest that the version of events has been rehearsed in some way.

Did the Police or ambulance attend the scene of the accident? One may wish to obtain the Police report or the ambulance records to check what the emergency services were told about the accident circumstances. If the investigation is commenced early enough, is there any CCTV footage or independent witnesses who may verify the Claimant's version of events?

It may be that one questions the credibility of a witness who says that a vehicle in front caused him to brake but the witness cannot recall any details about that vehicle such as the make, model or vehicle registration number, or even the colour of the vehicle. Also beware of passengers who all say they did not see the accident and all say they were talking on a mobile phone or the like, it may not be likely that they all did not witness the collision.

It may also be worth putting Part 18 Questions to the Defendant's insurer in such circumstances. For example if the Defendant says that the vehicle that caused the Claimant to brake was simply not there did the Defendant have a good view of the road ahead, could the Defendant's insurer simply have missed the vehicle that caused the Claimant to brake?

Was the Claimant's vehicle blocking the Defendant's insured's view and can the Defendant's insured be certain that the vehicle was not there?

How The Cases Are Won Or Lost At Trial

It is arguable that it is relatively rare for the Court to make a finding that the Claimant braked for no reason to induce a collision. Undoubtedly there are criminal gangs that engage in this type of activity and there have been a number of recent prison sentences for gangs inducing accidents on roundabouts.

However experience dictates that insurers make far more of these allegations than are ever made out at Trial. It is arguable that for Claimants the key to winning these cases at Trial is the credibility of the Claimant and in particular the plausibility of the Claimant's journey at the time of the collision and their credibility and plausibility of the reason for the Claimant to have braked.

For the Defendant, if the Defendant's insurer can identify significant inconsistencies in relation to the Claimant's version, has a credible policyholder, and in particular can impeach credibility in relation to the issue of causation, it is likely to make a strong Defence at Trial.

CHAPTER FIVE
PHANTOM PASSENGERS

Bogus Passenger Allegations: How Do They Arise?

It is a 4pm on a dark December evening. The Claimant has just picked his two young children up from school, who are five and six respectively. He is travelling home. He is stationary at traffic lights and the Defendant collides with the rear of his vehicle. The Defendant's driver gets out of the vehicle after the accident and walks over to the Claimant's vehicle. The Claimant's driver also gets out, they walk around to the back of the vehicle, examines the damage and exchange insurance details. The Defendant apologises and admits fault.

The day after the accident, the Claimant and his two young children start to experience neck and back pain. They attend the GP and are given painkillers. A week later the Claimant and his two children are still experiencing pain so they decide to make a claim for personal injury. They consult Solicitors, who think it will be a straightforward claim. The Solicitors send the Claimant and his children for GP reports. The claims are submitted to the low value portal and liability is admitted. The medical reports are submitted to the Defendant's insurer via the low value portal and offers of settlement are awaited.

A straightforward claim you may think? The Defendant's insurer writes to the Claimant's Solicitors after 10 weeks, saying they have concerns about the claim, but nothing more and refuse to disclose their concerns, pending further investigation. The claims are timed out of the low value portal. The Claimant's Solicitors issue Court proceedings for all three Claimants and a Defence is filed stating that there was only one child in the car, a female. They say therefore, one of the infants was not in the vehicle. Does this sound familiar?

Phantom passenger allegations, arguably, are becoming more and more prolific in personal injury litigation and the Defendant's insurers are holding back the nature of the allegation in more instances, until proceedings are issued.

How Can They Be Investigated?

The following provides some guidance as to how such allegations may be investigated quickly and efficiently:-

(a) Where were the Claimants going at the time of the accident? Was there a reason for all the Claimants to be in the vehicle? It is always worth obtaining any documentary evidence to confirm the reason for the journey.

For example, if the children were on the way home from school, obtain the school register to confirm their attendance at school.

If the Claimant has been shopping, do they have receipts for items they purchased and/or can they provide bank statements for items purchased?

If the Claimant was on the way home from work, can the employer confirm attendance on the day of the accident?

(b) Does the Claimant's journey make sense? It is plausible? Can the Claimant explain their route to where the accident happened, or where they were going?

Sometimes, the Claimant's statement, where a phantom passenger allegation is made will not explain this. Where fraud is being alleged it is extremely important the witness statement explains the reason for the journey in detail, together with the route taken and the relationship between all the parties within the vehicle. It is always worthwhile sending the Claimant a Google map and asking the Claimant to mark the map with the route to the destination.

(c) Credibility, Credibility, Credibility! They key to the success or failure of most cases is the Claimant's credibility. When the Defendant's insurer puts the allegation, it is extremely important to have a robust conference with Counsel to assess credibility.

Does the witness answer questions without hesitation? Is the witness evasive in their responses? Does the witness take the allegation seriously? Does the witness maintain eye contact when answering questions? Do the witness's responses lack detail or consistency? Some of these questions may raise red flags as to the credibility of the evidence.

If possible, get the Claimants into the office and put the allegation in person, to each Claimant separately, rather than over the telephone. The body language of the clamant will be extremely important when assessing credibility overall.

(d) Is there any other evidence that can verify the Claimant was at the scene of the accident? Are there any witnesses? Is there any CCTV? Did the police / ambulance attend and speak to the Claimant, and if so, is there a report that could place the Claimant in the vehicle?

Consider putting part 18 questions to the Defendant, to undermine the credibility of the evidence. Did the Defendant get a clear look into the vehicle? Was there anything blocking his view? Could the Claimant have got out of the vehicle, before he looked inside? Was it dark? Was the Defendant's eyesight poor? If he needs glasses, was he wearing them? If it was a small child, could the Defendant have missed the child in the car? Did the Defendant ever go over the Claimant's vehicle? Was he standing some distance away from the Claimant's vehicle? Did the Claimant's vehicle have tinted windows?

In order to find there was a phantom passenger with the vehicle, the Court will need to be sure that immediately after the collision, the Defendant walked over to the Claimant's vehicle, looked directly inside and is 100% sure the Claimant was not there, in the absence of some other objective evidence to show the Claimant could not have been at the scene of the accident.

It will be important to show the alleged phantom passenger did in fact sustain an injury as alleged.

i) Did the Claimant attend the GP/hospital? (obtain the notes)

ii) Did the Claimant have any time off work? (obtain evidence)

iii) Did the Claimant stop going to the gym? (obtain the records)

iv) Did the Claimant attend physiotherapy? (obtain the records)

All this evidence may provide some objectivity an injury was sustained as alleged, and can be persuasive to show the Claimant sustained an injury.

Does the Claimant's story fit? If the Claimant was at the scene of the accident, can they describe the other vehicle involved in the accident, i.e. the colour, make and model? Can they describe the other driver? Do they know the name of the road where the accident happened? Can they say what happened at the scene of the accident? Is this consistent with the other witnesses?

A witness who was genuinely at the scene of the accident (other than a younger child), should be able to provide you credible evidence on these points.

Conclusions

In *Shah v Ul-Haq & Ors [2009] EWCA Civ 542* (09 June 2009), the Court of Appeal held that there was no support in law for the proposition that a Claimant should be deprived of damages in his own claim, purely on the basis that he had supported a fraudulent claim made by another person. It was invariably the case that, where a claim had been dishonestly exaggerated, a Judge would award the limited damages that were appropriate to his findings, but would award the Claimant the damages to which he was indisputably entitled. There was no logical justification for suggesting that a Claimant who had lied about another person's claim should be treated any differently than someone who had lied about his own claim. However, if it is found that a Claimant has supported the claim of a phantom passenger, his costs are likely to be reduced accordingly.

Arguably, the key to winning alleged bogus passenger cases, as with any other type of alleged fraud is the credibility of the Claimant. Early evidential gathering is key while memories are fresh, together with detailed witness statements.

Arguably, an early and robust conference with Counsel is helpful as soon as the Defendant puts the allegation, to test the credibility of the Claimant's case, and before valuable time and money is spent investigating case that may otherwise fail at Trial, due to lack of credibility. Tactically, robust Part 18 questions will always work well with Defendant insurers and Solicitors, given many alleged phantom passengers cases are run and settled shorty before Trial, as the Defendant has not realised the weakness in it's own case.

Most alleged phantom passengers claims fail at Trial (for the Defendant), and there are few examples in law reports where the Defendant insurer has succeeded on such allegations, when one compares the number of cases where such allegations are made, as compared to the number that actually succeed at Trial.

CHAPTER SIX
CREDIT HIRE AND STORAGE FRAUD

Introduction

Credit hire and storage claims are proving some of the most difficult matters for Courts to adjudicate upon. With credit hire and storage fraud on the increase, Claimant and Defendant firms must be alive to this type of fraud and how to spot it. A poorly investigated or prepared hire or storage claim, can cause the Claimant enormous difficulties at Trial or Disposal. This chapter looks at some of the most common 'concerns' with hire and storage claims and how to tackle them.

Credit Hire and Storage Credibility Concerns?

- The hire or storage company does not exist.
- The hire company, appear to hire the same vehicle out, to two Claimants, at the same time i.e. one of the hire claims is bogus.
- The full period of hire claimed, did not take place.
- The vehicle alleged to have been hired, is not the vehicle actually hired to the Claimant. For example, the Claimant is provided with a less prestige vehicle, than the one claimed on the agreement.
- The hire company add extras onto the hire, such as Collision Damages Waiver, satellite navigation, insurance or an additional driver, and such services were not provided to the Claimant.
- The Claimant's vehicle is not stored for the period claimed.
- Bogus credit hire or storage companies sometimes linked to claims management companies and other types of RTA fraud.

- The Claimant did not sign the hire agreement or someone else other than the Claimant, signed the credit hire, or storage documents, and it is suggested they were signed by the Claimant.

- The hire company suggest that the agreement was signed at the office of the hire or storage company, when in fact it was signed at the Claimant's home address or place of work, to get around the Cancellation of Contract Regulations in a Consumers Home or Place of Work Regulations 2008.

- The hire vehicle, hired to the Claimant did not have valid road tax, an MOT certificate or credit hire insurance, so it should not have been hired to the Claimant, in the first instance.

- The hire company, do not own the hire car, so they are not entitled to hire the car out, as a credit hire car.

- If the hire vehicle hired, was a taxi, it did not have the correct license from the local authority or insurance to cover the credit hire vehicle, to be used for hire or reward, so it should not have been provided to the Claimant for use as a taxi.

Problems for the Claimant?

It may be argued that a problematic hire and storage claim, can affect the credibility, of an otherwise genuine claim. The Claimant may simply place the repairs or storage of the car into the hands of, what appears to be a genuine credit hire or storage company.

Some County Court Judges do not seem to favour credit hire and storage claims, especially where the claims are high value and it appears as though, the credit hire company is pressing or funding the litigation.

If a finding of fraud is made at Trial, the Claimant's ATE provider is unlikely to indemnify the claim, leaving the Claimant with a large costs bill, as well as potential criminal implications for the Claimant. The

Claimants Solicitor's costs recovery, are also likely to be limited in such circumstances.

If a hire or storage claim is found to be a sham at Trial, it is the Claimant who is likely to be ordered to pay the costs and not the credit hire, or storage company. The Claimant must be advised in relation to the prospects of success of the hire and storage claim, if foul play is suspected.

How Can This Type of Fraud be Detected By The Defendant?

Some of the enquiries the Defendant's insurer may undertake may be as follows:-

- Many insurance companies now log the dates of hire and vehicles hired, for all new credit hire claims submitted, so they can detect if a vehicle is claimed to have been hired to two Claimants, at the same time.

- The Defendant's insurance company may, instruct an investigator to visit the office of the hire, storage or claims management company, if it suspected the hire company or storage company does not exist. This information is then shared between insurance companies.

- The Defendant may make enquiries with the taxi licensing authority and local Council, to check the hire car had the appropriate license for public hire or reward.

- The VAT registration number of the hire and storage number can be checked to ensure it is genuine.

- Enquiries can also be made with the credit hire companies insurer, to check if the vehicle had valid insurance and online checks can be made to check the hire vehicle, had a valid MOT, at the time of hire.

- Enquiries can be made of the DVLA to check whether the hire company, was the registered keeper of the hire car.

What Can We Do to Prevent and Detect This Type of fraud?

The short answer is that both Claimant and Defendant Solicitors need to check and vet the hire and storage claims carefully, upon receipt of instructions.

Many Claimant firms receive personal injury referral cases, involving credit hire and storage claims, from credit hire, storage and claims management companies. It is prudent for the Claimant Lawyer to know where the work is coming from, and checks be undertaken to ensure it is a genuine source of work.

One should not assume the hire and storage agreements are correct. The Claimant's Solicitor can ensure that copies of the original credit hire and storage agreements are sent to the Claimant, at the outset and a statement is taken from the Claimant to confirm:-

(a) If the Claimant signed the hire/ storage agreement. If not, who did?

(b) When and where, the agreement was signed.

(c) If dates of the hire and storage are correct.

(d) If vehicles hired to the Claimant are correct.

(e) The address where the car was recovered to and stored, if applicable

(f) If any extras such as CDW, or satellite navigation, have been claimed correctly.

If there is any doubt, a statement should be obtained from the Claimant and the hire/ storage company, to explain any discrepancies.

If there is any doubt the hire or storage company exists, the hire actually took place, as per the agreement or the Claimant's vehicle was actually placed in storage, for the period claimed, an investigator can be instructed to attend the premises of the hire and storage company to undertake the following investigations:-

1. Obtain a signed statement from the credit hire company to confirm the vehicle(s) that were hired to the Claimant, where the hire agreement was signed, who signed it and the dates of hire.

2. Obtain photographs of the hire companies premises and hire vehicle(s) that were hired to the Claimant.

3. Obtain a signed statement from the storage company to confirm, the address where the Claimant's vehicle was stored, the dates it was stored from and to and if the storage company disposed of the vehicle, the full name and address of the person who it was sold, or passed on to.

4. Obtain photographs of the storage facility, preferably with the Claimant's damaged vehicle, if it is still in storage.

5. Obtain copies of the certificates of insurance, taxi licenses (if applicable), MOT certificates, V5 certificate or proof of ownership i.e. sales receipt and road tax badges, for all the vehicles hired to the Claimant.

The following verification checks on the hire company/storage company can also be undertaken: -

- Checks can be made of the VAT registration number of the hire and storage company online. This can be done at:-
http://ec.europa.eu/taxation_customs/vies/vieshome.do

- Checks can be made to ensure the credit hire car has a valid MOT certificate online. This can be done at:-

http://www.direct.gov.uk/en/Motoring/OwningAVehicle/Mot/DG_10020539

- A DVLA search can be carried out, to confirm if the hire company is the registered keeper of the hire vehicle. An application must be made to the DVLA explaining the reasons for the search.

- Checks can be made with the hire companies' insurer, to check if the hire vehicle had valid insurance at the time of the accident.

- Checks can be made with the taxi licensing authority (usually the department of the local authority) to check whether the vehicle had a valid taxi license, if it was used for hire or reward, as a hire vehicle.

Summary

It may be argued that those conducting credit hire and storage claims, where allegations of fraud are made, need to be particularly diligent. It is important that Claimant law firms, know the sources of work and validation checks are undertaken on new credit hire / storage firms, who are a source of personal injury work, even taking into account referral fees are now banned.

It may be argued that one should be particularly wary of sudden requests from an unknown credit hire firm who requests a Claimant law firm to take on large volumes of work, if the claims have other fraud indicators, discussed in other chapters. Further validation checks may be necessary, especially if the credit hire / storage claims look unprofessional i.e no VAT number on invoices, pro forma invoices, invoices that lack details such as the vehicle registration number or full details of the credit hire car registration number etc.

It may be argued that when taking instructions on such claims, is especially important that Claimant Lawyers, examine the documents submitted by the hire / storage company closely and these documents are checked with the lay client carefully, to check they are accurate and the original documents that were agreed/signed with the Claimant.

The growth of credit hire fraud is only likely to increase as insurers become more robust at investigating and identifying other types of fraud, and it is therefore prudent that those who are involved in this area of practice can identify fraud indicators and validate such claims, whether they be Claimant or Defendant practitioners.

CHAPTER SEVEN
FRAUD, BURDENS OF PROOF AND PLEADINGS (UPDATED 2016)

Do You Have To Prove Fraud?

In the majority of cases, it may be argued that there will be no need to prove fraud, even if there is sufficient evidence in order to plead it. In many cases, the Defendant's insurer will not want to plead the issue of fraud at Trial, unless it is the Defendant's insurer's intention to go after the Claimants for contempt of Court proceedings in the event of a finding of fraud by the Trial Judge.

The reason many Defendant's insurers will not want to plead the issue of fraud, and simply put the Claimant to strict proof in relation to the issues of breach of duty, causation and quantum, is that if the Trial Judge makes a finding of fraud, it is very unlikely the Claimant's after the event insurer, will indemnify the Claimant in relation to the issue of costs and the Defendant's insurer, even after winning a Trial on the issue of fraud, will be left to go after the Claimant for their costs and it is usually the case that the Claimants in these sorts of cases but not in all cases, have very little assets, property or other funds to cover the Defendant's costs bill and invariably the Defendant's insurer remains unable to recover their costs in some circumstances for these reasons.

It may be argued that for the Defendant's insurer in the majority of circumstances it may simply be better that Claimants' claims are dismissed on the balance of probability as failing to prove breach of duty, causation or quantum, rather than an outright finding of fraud by the Trial Judge.

The only exception to this, is likely to be where the Defendant's insurer wishes to obtain a Judgment for the purpose of deterring other fraudulent claims that is to be published and in this case a finding of fraud is necessary, and will need to be pleaded.

It is of course the case, that if the Defendant's insurer pleads fraud, then it must also prove the issue of fraud on the balance of probability, but even if the Defendant's insurer does not prove fraud, then the Claimant still has to meet the balance of probability test in the normal way.

When one looks at the reporting of fraudulent cases on the legal databases, one does find that there are very few reported decisions where findings of fraud have been made by the Trial Judge in the circumstances of staged/contrived collisions, slam on collisions or decoy vehicle accidents. It has to be argued, that this is certainly only a tiny proportion of reported cases which contain road traffic accidents with findings of fraud, as compared to the number of such allegations that are made by Defendant's insurers. The reason for this may well be the lack of Defendant's insurers reporting such cases where findings of fraud have been made, or it could be that the Courts are making relatively few findings on this basis.

It may be argued that the Courts, and especially Courts such as Central London and Birmingham, are becoming more readily prepared to make findings of fraud in cases, even on low velocity impact type allegations. It may be argued, that far more allegations of fraud cases, whether it be outright fraud or exaggeration, fail on the balance of probability test, as opposed to outright findings of fraud by the Court in relation to those allegations.

It therefore may be argued, that in relation to pleadings of fraud, it will usually be sufficient to set out the concerns and put the Claimant to strict proof on the balance of probability, rather than pleading fraud.

In the case of *Medcalf –v- Mandell* the House of Lords considered paragraph 704 of the Bar Code of Conduct and Barristers' Duties in considering whether or not to draft a document including an allegation of fraud. Paragraph 704(c) states that a Barrister *"should not draft a document containing an allegation of fraud unless he has clear instructions to make such an allegation and has before him reasonably credible material which as it stands establishes a prima facie case of fraud. In that case the Court of Appeal had taken the view that a Barrister in making such an allegation should have before him evidence which can be put before the Court to make good the allegation. The House of Lords rejected this interpretation and Lord Bingham of Cornhill said that "the requirement is not that Counsel should necessarily have before him evidence in admissible form but he should have material of such a character as to leave responsible Counsel to conclude that serious allegations should properly be based upon it".* The Bar Standards Board Guidance from September 2008 which says that although paragraph 704 refers specifically to fraud, the same principal would apply to any other allegation of serious misconduct.

The SRA Code of Conduct has similar principles embedded within it. It is therefore necessary, that before a Solicitor or Counsel puts his name to a pleading of fraud, and in particular a Defendant Solicitor signs a pleading of fraud, the relevant checks must be necessary to confirm that there is prima facie evidence which establishes a prima facie case of fraud. It is therefore prudent, that before any allegation is put by the Defendant's insurer in relation to issues such as occupancy/slam on or decoy vehicle type accidents, that there is a signed Statement of Truth from the policyholder confirming the allegations. It may be argued that if fraud is being pleaded by a Defendant's insurer, although the Defendant's Solicitor can sign the Statement of Truth on the Defence, it is preferable for the document to be signed by a senior representative of the Defendant insurance company as the Second Defendant and the policyholder or driver themselves as the First Defendant, so it is clear to the insurer and the driver or policyholder the basis upon which the allegations are being made.

The Balance Of Probability Test

It should be noted, that in the ordinary course of events, allegations of fraud cases will normally be determined upon the standard balance of probability test i.e. is it more likely than not that the accident occurred in the way that the Claimant said it did, the Claimant sustained an injury as a result of that collision, and it was a genuine accident.

However, in the case of Re H (A Minor) 1995 1FLR stated:-

> *"The balance of probability standard means that the Court is satisfied that an event occurred if it considers that, on the evidence the occurrence of the event was more likely than not. When assessing the probabilities the Court will have in mind the factor to whatever extent is appropriate in the particular case, that the more serious the allegation the less likely it is that the event occurred and hence, the stronger should be the evidence before the Court concludes that the allegation is established on the balance of probability. Fraud is usually less likely that negligence. Deliberate physical injury is likely than accidental physical injury. A step father is usually less likely to have repeatedly raped and had non consensual oral sex with his under age step daughter than on the same occasion to have lost his temper and slapped her. It builds into the preponderance of probability standard is a generous degree of flexibility in respect of the seriousness of the allegation.*
>
> *Although the result is much the same, this does not mean that where a serious allegation is in issue, the standard of proof required is higher. It means that the inherent probability or improbability of an event is itself a matter to be taken into account when weighing the probabilities and deciding whether, on the balance, the event occurred. The more improbable the event, the stronger must be the evidence that it did occur before, on the balance of probability its occurrence will be established".*

It may therefore be argued, that where the Defendant pleads fraud, or simply sets out a series of concerns on a strict proof Defence, the evidential burden for the Defendant of proving those allegations will be higher given the seriousness of those allegations.

Civil Procedure Rules 16.5

CPR 16.5 sets out as follows:-

> *"1. In his Defence the Defendant must state:-*
>
> *(a) Which of the allegations in the Particulars of Claim he denies;*

(b) Which allegations he is unable to admit or deny but which requires the Claimant to prove; and

(c) Which allegations he admits.

2. Where the Defendant denies an allegation:-

(a) He must state his reasons for doing so; and

(b) If he intends to put forward a different version of events from that given by the Claimant, he must state his own version of events.

3. A Defendant who:-

(a) Fails to deal with an allegation; but

(b) Has set out in his Defence the nature of his case in relation to the issue to which that allegation is relevant shall be taken to require the allegation to be proved".

It may be argued, that this part of the CPR, is particularly useful when considering the issue of Defendant's insurers who plead fairly vague strict proof Defences in relation to their "concerns about the case". For example, if the Defendant pleads a Defence which says no Police attendance at the accident, no witnesses and the Claimant has had a number of previous accidents, or there are address links to the Claimant's address from other claims, then it may be argued that it is not a Defence which complies with CPR 16.5. It may be argued, that with prevalence of allegations of fraud cases, the Courts are becoming less tolerant of vague Defences which plead vague concerns about accidents. For example if the Police did not attend the accident or there are no independent witnesses, it may be argued that there are many such genuine accidents for example straightforward liability disputes where the Police or witnesses do not attend the accident.

It may be argued that under CPR 16.5 the Defendant should set out in detail the relevant allegations in relation to the Claimant's case, so that the Claimant may appropriately reply to the allegations in a Reply to the Defence.

It could be argued that relevant to this issue, is guidance given by Lord Justice Davies in *Hussain –v- Amin and Charters Insurance Limited 2012 EWCA Civ 1456* where he stated:-

> *"I would however particularly wish to add my own comments about the pleaded Defence of the Second Defendant. It was perfectly proper to join issue on the primary facts alleged in the Particulars of Claim and as to whether there had indeed been any negligence on whether the claim losses had been caused thereby. But the pleaded Defence went much further in paragraph 7 and 9 setting out a number of matters which, if it was alleged raised significant concerns as to the possibility or not this had been a staged accident requiring further investigation. Possibly, although I may have reservations, such a pleading could be justified as an initial holding Defence. But it is a case pleaded on insinuation not allegation. If the Second Defendant considers that it has sufficient material to justify a plea that the claim was based on a collision which was a sham or a fraud, it behoathed in properly and in ample time before Trial so as to plead it in clear and unequivocal terms and with proper particulars. Thereafter the burden of proof would of course have been on the Second Defendant to establish such a Defence.*
>
> *In the event, as I see it, the Claimant was faced with a hybrid, in effect was being required at Trial to deal with an insinuation of fraud without any express allegation to that effect pleaded. Realistically the Trial Judge who dealt with the matter in the round, concluded that the claim was not fabricated or fraudulent and the accident had not been staged. But this sort of pleading should not be sanctioned. It is in fact something of an irony that the Second Defendant seeks to criticise the conduct of the Claimant's Solicitors,*

> *when in part at least they were having to deal with an abusive Defence".*

Again it may be argued, that although these comments were Obiter, it is an indication that the Court are now less prepared to deal with Defences based upon insinuations that a claim may be fraudulent, rather than on properly pleaded allegations. If a Claimant Lawyer receives any such Defences from a Defendant's insurer, the case it may be argued is worth pleading in a Reply to a Defence and potentially in support of an Application to strike out any such Defence.

Reply To The Defence

CPR 16.7 sets out as follows:-

> *"1. A Claimant who does not file a Reply to the Defence shall not be taken to admit the matters raised in the Defence.*
>
> *2. A Claimant who files a Reply to the Defence but fails to deal with the matter raised in the Defence shall be taken to require the matter to be proved".*

It is prudent in cases where concerns or allegations or insinuations of fraud are raised by the Defendant's insurers that a proper Reply to the Defence is filed at the earliest possible stage.

It may be argued that this is necessary in circumstances where allegations are made, as it not only sets out the Claimant's position at an early stage, but focuses the parties' minds in relation to the issues being raised and how to rebut them.

Therefore, it may be argued that a Reply to the Defence is an extremely useful tool, not only in setting out the relevant responses to the allegations which should be dealt with in detail, but it also allows the Claimant to make early disclosure requests in relation to matters pleaded in the Defence. For example, if a Defence raises issues such as indemnity, allegations in relation to various data searches that have been undertaken on the Claimant, and the like, then the Claimant should make requests for disclosure of these documents in the Reply to the Defence, and then if not disclosed after or by standard disclosure stage, it makes it easier for the Claimant to file and be successful in relation to an Application for specific disclosure under CPR 31.12.

The Particulars of Claim

Finally, a brief word is mentioned in relation to the Particulars of Claim. It may be argued, that it is a sad fact of modern road traffic litigation, that many pleadings have now become "factory processed" and not as much thought and care is in some cases, going into drafting the Particulars of Claim. However, if the Claimant is likely to be faced with an allegation of fraud at Trial, it is essential that the Particulars of Claim should be carefully drafted. It may be argued, that in particular one may wish to pay particularly close attention, to the accident circumstances to make sure these are correct, and also the allegations of negligence and breach of duty are also correct. On occasion, one can sometimes find that when these documents are drafted without thought and care, accident circumstances can be stated incorrectly, and/or allegations of negligence are not set out correctly. The Claimant is later cross examined on these documents at Trial and has no explanation.

It may be argued, that where an allegation of fraud is being put by the Defendant's insurer, it is prudent that the Claimant signs the Particulars of Claim as opposed to the Claimant's Lawyer to ensure the factual accuracy of the document, and also that the Claimant has been given the correct warnings, in relation to the consequences of signing a Particulars of Claim or any other pleading for that matter, where the Claimant does not have an honest belief in the truth of the document.

It may further be argued, that this is again particularly prudent where the Claimant's first language is not English and it is vitally important that the Particulars of Claim in those circumstances contains a correct translation clause and the document is signed by somebody who speaks the Claimant's language, and is independent of the case in ideal circumstances.

The Schedule of Loss

Where the Claimant is bringing a personal injury claim, the CPR sets out that the Claimant must attach a separate Schedule of Loss if claiming for special damages. Again, especially if allegations of fraud are being made by the Defendant's insurers or concerns are being made out by the Defendant's insurers, it is prudent that the Schedule of Loss is sent to the Claimant to sign, together with all of the documents relied on by the Claimant in terms of special damages i.e. copies of the credit hire agreement, physiotherapy invoices, storage invoices etc, if applicable.

The reasoning for this, follows the decision in *Fairclough Homes Limited –v- Summers 2002 UKSC 26*. This was a case, where the Defendant's insurers alleged that the Claimant had exaggerated a claim for personal injury including verifying Statements of Truth which were not correct. Following a Trial on quantum in January 2010 the Trial Judge found *"that the evidence before me is sufficiently cogent to sustain a claim of fraud not only applying the civil standard of being satisfied on the balance of probability but also on the criminal standard of being satisfied beyond reasonable doubt".*

If the Defendant is alleging exaggeration, as will be in the case of any allegation of a low speed impact, or is alleging that the credit hire claim or storage claim is exaggerated in any way, then it is prudent that the Claimant signs the Schedule of Loss and has an opportunity to check the document in detail before it is signed.

It is arguable, that some alleged fraud cases, in some instances for the Defendant, fail on the primary allegations of fraud, but it can be found that a Claimant has exaggerated a case, either in relation to injury or items of special damages, and therefore the Claimant's damages and particularly costs in such circumstances are likely to be reduced accordingly. The Claimant's lawyer therefore must check the schedule of special damage is 100% correct according to the Claimant's instructions before it is signed. This is particularly relevant to credit hire and storage claims, and it is prudent for the Claimant to check these to confirm their authenticity before the schedule is signed, especially if the documents are sent to the Solicitors, directly by the hire/storage company, and do not come from the Claimant directly.

Case in Burden of Proof

In (1) MOHAMED RIZAN (2) MOHAMMED RILSHAD v (1) BARRY HAYES (2) ALLIANZ INSURANCE PLC (2016) [2016] EWCA Civ 481, the Court found that although a judge had been wrong to state that a claim for damages from a road traffic accident had been fraudulent, he had been entitled to dismiss the claim without making a finding of fraud. The judge had not been faced with a binary choice between fraud and the accident as alleged, and the claimants had failed to discharge the burden of proof. The Court initially found:-

> *"1. This is a claim for damages for personal injury and consequential loss brought by Messrs Mohamed Rizan and Mohamed Wilshad (who are I think gentlemen of Tamil origin, I am not sure whether Indian or Sri Lankan) who have been in England for quite some time and who both describe themselves as part-time taxi drivers.*
>
> *2. On 17th September 2008 (i.e. getting on for six years ago), the contention is that there was a collision between a BMW 7 Series motor car, which was being driven by the First Claimant, and an Astra Van driven by Mr Hayes who is the First Defendant. It should be said that Mr Hayes has played no part in this trial and the interests of the Allianz Insurance Company have been dealt with by it becoming a party and dealing with the Claimants' claim itself.*
>
> *3. Efforts were made, it appears, to get Mr Hayes to come to Court; he was visited by an Inquiry Agent, Mr Walton, a Claims Investigator, who took a statement from him. Another statement had been taken from him, but he has stoutly resisted the temptation to come to Court to give evidence.*

4. *What the Claimant says happened, broadly speaking, is that he was driving along a road called Park Road, which seems to be something of a rural road although running between Beaconsfield and Slough. It was, it appears, in the evening at about 8pm. The BMW was going towards Slough and an Astra Van, which it is said was driven by the First Defendant, came down Church Lane from the left of the BMW. The situation is illustrated in many plans and photographs. It emerged without stopping, colliding with the side of the BMW.*

5. *The reading of the Statement of Claim, an account given in the medical report, the Further and Better Particulars and the Claimant's own statement give no indication whatever that the car being driven by the First Claimant was doing anything other than driving at 30 to 40 mph at the time of the accident, as it passed the mouth of Church Lane. If it was doing that, it is inconceivable that the damage which has been seen by the engineer instructed by the Defendant could have occurred then, because the damage to the BMW was simply indentations to both the doors on the nearside and there was no, as it were, lateral damage before or after these areas of indentations.*

6. *Both of the engineers in a joint statement agreed:*

   "The photographs of the passenger side of the BMW show vertical marks within the damage. No horizontal marks are apparent. In a collision in which the front of a van contacts the passenger side of a car travelling at 35 to 40mph, we would certainly expect to see substantial horizontal marks and damage extending alongside of the car, in this case the BMW. The width of the damage to the side of the BMW matches the width of the front of the van".

   Both experts concluded that, on the balance of probability, the car must have been stationary at the time of impact.

7. *This the Claimant attempts to deal with when he comes to give evidence today by saying that he was indeed stationary at the time.*

He had seen this car coming and braked as hard as he could. His car (he said) was stopped at the point of the impact in the middle of the junction and he was hit on the left-hand passenger side.

8. *There are difficulties about that from the point of view of stopping distance and reaction times and visibility, into which it is probably not necessary for me to go in any details save that it would have been extremely marginal, if the speed had been anything above 30mph, to have been able to stop from 35mph or so before the point of impact. But the significant point is that nowhere in the Letter before Action, the Statement of Claim, the account given to the Doctor or in the Claimants' own statement or in the Further and Better Particulars, was it thought appropriate for Mr Rizan to explain what he has now explained; that he had actually stopped.*

9. *One should make some slight allowance for language in this case; Mr Rizan is not a native English speaker, but his English is certainly perfectly serviceable and although a translator or interpreter was engaged, her services were not actually needed. I am quite satisfied that had Mr Rizan been saying all along that he braked as hard as he could and stopped and then been hit, that would have been reflected in the papers. What seems to have happened is that once it was appreciated that the engineering evidence was such that his case simply could not be right on the basis that it was being advanced, then the case altered.*

10. *Curiously enough, his passenger did not alter his evidence and he maintained that the car was still going at 35mph or 40mph, at the time of the accident. He did so both in Further and Better Particulars and in evidence. Not, it should be said, that one has the greatest of confidence in the evidence given by the Second Claimant since he had apparently been involved in some ten motor car collisions between August 2007 and March 2011, an incidence of accidents which he had taken some steps to avoid revealing when asked about.*

11. *The case had to proceed without any evidence being given by Mr Hayes, because he did not come. But Mr Hayes' statements were put before the Court in the form of exhibits to what Mr Walton said. Mr Hayes in his statement said that he was alone in his van, he was dropping off a friend of a friend, but did not know his name, and he thinks he:*

"...sort of slipped off the brake. I wasn't taking enough attention", And then said:

"The Claimant's car was going from my right to my left, hard to tell the speed in the dark"

Incidentally, the Claimant said it was not dark:

"He was going at 30 or 40 mph, something like that. Basically, he didn't have a chance to stop as I went straight out at him".

13. ***"In those circumstances, this is a case in which I cannot possibly be satisfied that the account given by the Claimant is a satisfactory account and in those circumstances this claim fails.***

14. *It is perhaps right to observe that it has, as one might expect perhaps given the antiquity of this case, come to trial before.* ***On 5th July 2012 it appears that a trial started. It is not quite clear what happened, but the Defendants I think (probably the Second Defendants) said that they wanted to allege fraud and for some reason the whole trial was abandoned in order to enable this to be done and for further investigations to take place.*** *It has taken getting on two years since then for this case to get back before the Court. It is a wholly unsatisfactory piece of litigation"*

On Appeal the Court found:-

38. *"In the present case the Claimants were seeking a judgment against the First Defendant Mr Hayes and not against the Second Defendant underwriters, but nothing turns on that. Mr Hayes took*

no part in the trial and the Claimants were obliged to prove their case against him. The only evidence adduced to the effect that these two vehicles had come into collision at the time and in the circumstances alleged came from the Claimants themselves. As the judge observed at paragraph 11, no evidence was given by Mr Hayes. By that he meant that Mr Hayes had given no evidence either orally or in the shape of a witness statement admitted in evidence pursuant to the Civil Evidence Act 1995 and the Rules of Court made thereunder. As the judge quite correctly noted by his formulation in paragraph 12 of his judgment, referring to what Mr Hayes is reported as having said, the two witness statements of Mr Hayes which he read were not admissible in evidence as proof of what was stated therein. Mr Patterson acknowledged that there was before the judge no admissible evidence from Mr Hayes. The conclusion of the experts that the two vehicles had come into collision albeit at a time when the BMW was stationary does not assist in tying the impact to the circumstances and place alleged. I would also emphasise that stationary means not moving, not slow or almost stationary, which is what the Claimants alleged in their Reply was the state of the BMW at the moment of impact. Thus the court needed to be satisfied that the evidence of the Claimants as to the occurrence of the accident was reliable evidence upon which it could make findings of fact on the balance of probability.

39. ***The judge gave his reasons for regarding the evidence before him as unreliable and we would not be justified in interfering with that conclusion unless we regarded it as a conclusion to which no reasonable judge could have come. Far from being so persuaded I find the judge's reasons, with one exception, cogent and compelling. At the very least the judge's conclusion falls well within the ambit of reasonable decision-making.***

40. *I agree with Mr Patterson that the fact that Mr Walton observed two gentlemen of Indian appearance leaving Mr Hayes' house when he visited him four years after the alleged accident was of no probative value. More to the point however was that, as the judge pointed out, Mr Hayes did not know the name of one of his alleged*

friends. The short point however is that the judge was right to recognise that Mr Hayes' witness statements were not evidence of the matters stated therein, and right moreover to record that Mr Hayes' reported account of the accident was inconsistent with the agreed accident reconstruction evidence. The judge might have added that Mr Hayes' reported account was also inconsistent in important respects with what had become the Claimants' evidence. In his statement given to Mr Walton Mr Hayes said that the BMW "carried on along the road" after the accident and that "they managed to stop their car on the left up the road after the accident." He said that he had not gone to look at the damage to the other vehicle because "the other car stopped too far up the road after the accident." This is obviously inconsistent with the BMW being stationary at the point of impact.

42. *Mr Patterson was critical of the judge's reasons for regarding the Second Claimant as an unreliable witness. First, he said that the judge had overlooked his evidence in re- examination. In re-examination Mr Jackson asked him:*

". . . your evidence has been that at the time of the accident you were travelling at 30 miles an hour. At the time of the impact, when the two vehicles touched, collided, what speed were you travelling then?"

To which his answer was:

"There's no travelling, the car stopped at zero speed. The car at the moment the car hit everything stopped. All I can see was the car on the left hand side, this car's there, that's all I can see."

I do not agree that that answer assists the Claimants. It is not an answer to the effect that the BMW had braked in anticipation of an impact and that by the time of the impact the car was stationary. We must also remember that the judge saw and heard the witnesses give their evidence, an advantage denied to us. I have already set out, at paragraph 10 above, how this point about speed before impact and speed at impact was sought to be rationalised by the Claimants in their Reply, which was a precursor to how the First Claimant at any rate sought to put it in evidence at trial. I find the attempted rationalisation acutely unconvincing, and that is plainly how it struck the judge, even after he had made due allowance for English not being the First Claimant's native tongue.

43. ***Mr Patterson also suggested that the fact that the Second Claimant appeared to have been involved in an unusually high number of accidents, ten in less than four years, was of itself a "weak" reason for not accepting his evidence. That was not however the judge's reason for lacking confidence in his evidence. The judge's reason was the Second Claimant's apparent anxiety that his unfortunate record should not come to light. That is a telling point.***

44. *Accordingly I would uphold the judge's dismissal of the Claimants' claims".*

CHAPTER EIGHT
DRAFTING IN ALLEGATIONS OF FRAUD CASES, PRE-ACTION DISCLOSURE APPLICATIONS AND DISCLOSURE

Witness Statements

It is arguable, that the Witness Statement is likely to be the most important document in the entire case for both the Claimant and the Defendant. It may be argued, that an entire case can turn upon the contents of the Witness Statements, and therefore it may be argued that it is extremely important that the Witness Statement is carefully drafted and a great deal of attention and care goes into the drafting of the Witness Statements. It may be argued that some of the following points may be relevant in relation to the drafting of Statements.

(a) CPR 32 Practice Direction 20.1 says *"a Witness Statement is the equivalent of the oral evidence that the witness would, if called, give in evidence, it must include a Statement by the intended witness that he believes the facts in it are true"*.

(b) Further CPR 32 Practice Direction 18.1 says *"the Witness Statement must be practical be in the intended witnesses own words, the Statements should be expressed in the first person and should also state the full name of the witness, his place of residence or if he is making the Statement in his professional business or other occupational capacity the address at which he worked, the position he holds and the name of his firm or employer"*.

(c) Further CPR 32 Practice Direction 18.2 says *"a Witness Statement must indicate which of the Statements in it are made from the witnesses' own knowledge and which are matters of information or belief and the sources of any matters of information or belief"*.

The Civil Procedure Rules, therefore make it perfectly clear that Statements should be in a witnesses' own words. It can be therefore argued, that a Witness Statement should not be argumentative, it should not contain legal submissions, and it should not be drafted in a Lawyer's language.

The key point of a Witness Statement, is to elicit evidence in the Claimant's own words, and it may be argued that it is vitally important that the Witness Statements taker does not seek to influence the contents of the witnesses' evidence in any way. The Statement taker should simply record the evidence as dictated by the witness.

The Lawyer, should not seek to influence the contents of the Statement, and it may well be that the language adopted by the witness is not agreeable with the Statement taker, but the Lawyer should not seek to change the language of the Statement and this should be reflected in the witnesses' own words. If one looks at a Trial Bundle, it quickly becomes evident if a Witness Statement has been drafted in the Lawyer's language and not that of the witness.

It may be argued that one should remember that ultimately the Claimant or the witness is likely to be cross examined on the contents of the Witness Statement and it is the witness who has to sign the Statement of Truth on the document to confirm the facts are true to the best of the witnesses' knowledge and belief. It is of no assistance to the Claimant, to the parties or to the Court if the Witness Statement is therefore misleading because it has been drafted in a way that is not agreeable to the witness.

It is further prudent, to take a Statement in a logical format, from the beginning of the accident I.e. from the moment that the Claimant sets off to the conclusion of the collision and the parties leaving the scene after the accident and all of the events in between. It is acceptable for a Witness Statement taker to ask open ended questions in order to encourage the Claimant to elicit the relevant information. Often one will find that when a Statement is taken the witness will instantly want to relay all the facts of the accident sometimes in a non logical order. It is up to the Statement taker to direct the witness to answer the questions in a logical manner so the Statement flows if possible in a chronological manner, first of all dealing with the issue of liability followed by causation and quantum.

It may be argued, that it is important that the Witness Statement addresses all of the issues in the Defence and sets out the responses to any allegations made in the Defence. However, a Witness Statement is not designed to be used for legal submissions or legal arguments and these should be confined to the Reply to the Defence or to the Skeleton Argument in preparation for Trial.

It could be argued, that a poorly drafted Witness Statement is likely to severely affect the credibility of the case and placed under cross examination. It is therefore essential, that the Witness Statement is drafted carefully and preferably by the fee earner with conduct of the case. It not only allows the fee earner with conduct of the case to familiarise oneself with the evidence, but it also allows the Claimant's Lawyer to spot any weaknesses or inconsistencies in the case that are going to cause problems later on at the Trial. One sometimes finds that where Statements are delegated to third parties to draft as sometimes happens in respect of economics, fee earners it may be argued sometimes miss key points due to the fact somebody else has taken the Statement.

<u>Non English Speaking Claimants</u>

It may be argued, that particular care needs to be taken with regards to non English speaking Claimants. It is essential, that if the Claimants' first language is not English or indeed the Claimant only has broken English, then an independent translator should be used to take the Witness Statement. In relation to inability of persons to read or sign documents to be verified by a Statement of Truth CPR 22 Practice Direction 3(a)(i) says:

> *"where a document containing a Statement of Truth is to be signed by a person who is unable to read or sign the document it must contain a certificate made by an authorised person. An authorised*

person is a person who is able to administer oaths and take Affidavits but needs not be independent of the parties or their representatives. The authorised person must certify:-

(a) That the document had been read to the person signing it.

(b) That the person appeared to understand it and approved its contents as accurate.

(c) That the declaration of truth has been read to that person.

(d) That person appeared to understand the declaration and the consequences of making a false declaration.

(e) That person signed or made his mark in the presence of the authorised person".

The format of the declaration appears in the Practice Direction to CPR 22 Statements of Truth. It is therefore essential, that if a Claimant cannot read or write English or speak the language or there is evidence of broken English, then an appropriate translator should translate the document for the Claimant and verify that the document has been read over to the Claimant by signing the appropriate translation certificate, following completion of the translation.

It may be argued, that it is not appropriate that this person is either another Claimant involved in the same accident, and any person from the accident management or hire company, and ideally this should be a professional independent translator if possible. It may be argued that the fees of such a person should be recoverable. Although not mandatory, it may also be prudent for the Statement to be translated into the Claimant's own language to ensure the accuracy of the translation, again by an independent translator. The same of course would apply for Part 18 Responses and any other pleadings to be signed by the Claimant.

It may be argued that in an allegation of fraud case, although technically it is possible for the Claimant's legal representative to sign a Reply to a Defence or a Response to a Part 18 Request, it is prudent that the Claimant has an opportunity to consider the pleadings before they are signed, and preferably the Claimant should be asked to sign a Statement of Truth on the document after checking them, particularly where there are serious allegations of fraud. It may also be argued, that this is especially prudent where there are language difficulties and the Claimant's representatives need to ensure that the Claimant has understood the Statements of Truth.

If one looks at the case of *Abdulla Ahmed Rasoul v (1) Giedrilis Linkevicius (2) Groupama Insurance Co Ltd (2012)* referred to elsewhere in this book, it may be argued that it is especially prudent that Statements are taken prior to the issue of Court proceedings, and in particular to ensure that the Claimant has understood the nature of the Defendant's allegations, and is able to respond appropriately to them. Arguably, this should also mean that any letters of advice to the Claimant in relation to pleadings including Statements and the Part 18 Questions, should also be translated into the Claimant's own language, preferably by an independent translator if there is nobody in the firm that speaks the Claimant's own language.

It should be borne in mind, that if a Claimant recklessly or deliberately signs a Statement of Truth the Claimant knows to be false, then this may lead to an Application for contempt of Court which can lead to a fine and/or imprisonment. It is therefore essential that all documents are translated, particularly where there is any doubt over the Claimant's ability to understand the contents of a Statement of Truth or the pleadings being signed.

Disclosure

In comparison to Part 18 Requests, both the Claimant and the Defendant can be compelled to provide disclosure before proceedings are issued. In some circumstances, it may be prudent to make a formal request for Pre-Action Disclosure of the Defendant pursuant to Part

31.16 if the Defendant alleges fraud or will not disclose why they are investigating the claim. It is argued, that sometimes one of the frustrations for Claimant Lawyers at the pre litigation stage of proceedings, is that the Defendant will not provide disclosure of relevant documentation until such time as proceedings are issued, because either investigations are ongoing in relation to the indemnity or the circumstances of the accident.

If the Defendant's insurers, will not give anything away in relation to the circumstances of the collision, or why there are ongoing concerns or indemnity concerns, it may be argued that the Claimant may wish to ask for disclosure of the following documentation:-

(a) The Defendant's engineer's report and/or repair invoice to determine damage consistency between the vehicles.

(b) Photographs of the damage to the Defendant's vehicle, even if the Defendant alleges that there was no damage to the vehicles, in order to determine the issue of damage consistency, and consider the possibility of a forensic engineer's report.

(c) A copy of the accident report form. It may be argued that this is not a privileged document, until the CNF form has been received.

(d) MOT Certificate for the Defendant's vehicle

(e) Any independent witness questionnaires. It should be noted that there is no property in a witness.

(f) Any data searches such as CUE (previous accidents), MIAFTR (previous total losses) or any other data searches undertaken on the Claimant such as Experian searches.

If the Defendant refuses disclosure the Claimant may wish to consider an Application for Pre-Action Disclosure under 31.16. It can be argued that where the Court will consider an Order for disclosure will depend upon the facts of the case. However it may be argued that the engineering and photographs are likely to be ordered in such circumstances, particularly if there is an argument between the parties over damage consistency.

Similarly, the Defendant's insurer may wish to make various disclosure requests of the Claimant at a pre litigation stage. This may include, the photographs of the damage to the vehicle and/or the engineering evidence especially an assessor's report in order to consider the issue of forensic engineering evidence.

It may be argued, that tactically, Claimants can sometimes be put under pressure in relation to litigation by their disclosure obligations. If there is a credit hire claim, the Claimant should be asked to disclose the following documents:-

(a) Confirmation of the MOT for the credit hire vehicle and the vehicle damaged in the accident to check it was roadworthy.

(b) The insurance certificate for the Claimant's vehicle and the hire vehicle to check that the vehicles were properly insured.

(c) Evidence that both vehicles had appropriate road tax to check that they were legally on the road at the time of the accident.

(d) If the Claimant was a taxi driver, a copy of the taxi licence.

(e) Impecuniosity documents including the Claimant's wage slips for a period of three months prior to the accident up to and including the end of the hire period together with loss of earnings information and if the Claimant was self employed profit and loss accounts and tax returns for the previous three years including covering the period of hire.

(f) Disclosure of financial information, may also be useful if the Claimant has stated to the medical expert that he took time off work as a result of the accident even if there was no formal loss of earnings claim, disclosure of financial records and letters and the

Claimant's personnel records should be obtained in order to confirm this.

(g) It is often the case that Claimants will state to the medical expert that they were unable to attend the gym, play snooker or participate in other leisure activities as a result of the accident. Very often such leisure facilities will keep records such as snooker clubs or the gym especially with the aid of electronic records. In such circumstances where the Claimant asserts he was unable to attend the gym for a period of time or go to the snooker club, then forms of authority for disclosure of the various records from the snooker club or gym etc should be sought from the Claimant and if refused the Defendant's insurer may consider an Application for specific disclosure under CPR 31.12.

In a similar way, if it is known that the Claimant has been involved in previous road traffic accidents, or the Claimant has made previous personal injury claims, then copies of all the medical reports should be sought from the Claimant together with full GP and hospital records and also physiotherapy records if available.

A recent tactic of Defendant practitioners is in such circumstances also to seek copies of any pleadings, Witness Statements or engineering evidence for any accidents that the Claimant has previously been involved in. This is an Order that Courts and particularly Central London County Court are prepared to make in such circumstances. It may be argued that it is therefore a useful tactic for Defendant practitioners to seek disclosure of all of the documents in relation to any previous or subsequent accidents the Claimant may have been involved in where fraud is alleged including but not limited to pleadings, engineering evidence, details of any settlements reached, Part 18 Responses, medical evidence etc. This of course can be a powerful tool in the Defendant's armoury when seeking to undermine the issue of the Claimant's credibility at Trial particularly if the Claimant has answered Part 18 Questions in relation to those issues.

CHAPTER NINE
FRAUD AND COSTS INCLUDING QADER V ESURE AND BROADHURST PART 36 OFFERS (UPDATED 2016)

Fixed Costs Portal and None Portal for Cases After 31 July 2013

A copy of the new costs Matrix for portal cases and fixed costs cases on or after 31 July 2013 is shown below. These tables are reproduced from:

http://www.justice.gov.uk/downloads/publications/policy/moj/rta-pi-scheme.pdf

ANNEX A

MOJ PROPOSED FIXED RECOVERABLE COSTS FOR CLAIMS WITHIN THE RTA AND EL/PL PROTOCOLS

	Claims of £1k-£10k			Claims of £10k-£25k		
	Stage 1	Stage 2	Total	Stage 1	Stage 2	Total
RTA claims	£200	£300	£500	£200	£600	£800
EL/PL claims	£300	£600	£900	£300	£1,300	£1,600

ANNEX B

MOJ PROPOSED FIXED RECOVERABLE COSTS FOR RTA, EL AND PL CLAIMS OUTSIDE THE RTA AND EL/PL PROTOCOLS

	Pre issue £1,000-£5,000	Pre Issue £5,001-£10,000	Pre Issue £10,001-£25,000	Issued – Post issue Pre Allocation	Issued – Post allocation pre listing	Issued – Post listing pre trial	Trial - Advocacy Fee
	Case Settles before Issue	Case Settles before Issue	Case Settles before Issue				
Road Traffic Accident							
Fixed Costs	Greater of £550 or £100 + 20% of Damages	£1,100 +15% of Damages over £5k	£1,930 + 10% of Damages over £10k	£1,160 + 20% of Damages	£1,880 + 20% of Damages	£2,655 + 20% of Damages	£485 (to £3,000) £690 (£3-10,000) £1,035 (£10-15,000) £1,650 (£15,000+)
Escape	+ 20%	+ 20%	+ 20%	+ 20%	+ 20%	+ 20%	n/a
Employers Liability							
Fixed Costs	£950 + 17.5% of Damages	£1,855 +12.5% of Damages over £5k	£2,500 + 10% of Damages over £10k	£2,630 + 20% of Damages	£3,350 + 25% of Damages	£4,280 + 30% of Damages	£485 (to £3,000) £690 (£3-10,000) £1,035 (£10-15,000) £1,650 (£15,000+)
Escape	+ 20%	+ 20%	+ 20%	+ 20%	+ 20%	+ 20%	n/a
Public Liability							
Fixed Costs	£950 +17.5% of Damages	£1,855 +10% of Damages over £5k	£2.370 + 10% of Damages over £10k	£2,450 + 17.5% of Damages	£3,065 + 22.5% of Damages	£3,790 + 27.5% of Damages	£485 (to £3,000) £690 (£3-10,000) £1,035 (£10-15,000) £1,650 (£15,000+)
Escape	+ 20%	+ 20%	+ 20%	+ 20%	+ 20%	+ 20%	n/a

Notes: Base fees - in all cases increased by 12.5% where London firm as per CPR 45

So What Does All This Mean for Allegations of Fraud Work?

- Some firms will choose no longer to undertake this area of work
- If alleged fraud cases stay in the fast track after 31 July 2013 it may be difficult to run them profitably within fixed costs.
- Cases that go to the multi-track, not stuck within fixed costs.

- Ask for a CMC to persuade the Court to put the case into the multi-track with oral submissions i.e see CPR 26.8, more than five witnesses, case likely to last for more than 1 day, need to call oral expert evidence i.e forensic engineers.

What if Alleged Fraud Cases Stay in the Fast Track, Could They Still Be Profitable Under Fixed Costs Post 31 July 2013?

The answer is yes but consider:-

A) Can You Obtain Indemnity From the Client's Bte Insurer?

See *Brown-Quinn & Another -v- Equity Syndicate Management Limited & Another [2012] EWCA Civ 1633.*

Facts

Ms Brown-Quinn, the respondent, had a policy of LEI with Equity Syndicate Management Limited, the appellant. The contract of insurance provided that should the respondent need the assistance of a legal representative, that representative was bound to work under terms provided for the appellant. The appellant had a number of solicitors whom they used on a regular basis. Amongst those terms was a clause that stated that the representative would only be paid at an agreed rate (this was £125 per hour). A further term was that, should the appointed representative cease to act or be dismissed by the respondent, the insurance would end unless the appellant agreed to another representative acting on her behalf. The respondent wished to pursue an employment claim and chose to fund this matter using her LEI. She selected a solicitor who did not work regularly for the appellant and the firm did not agree to act on the terms provided by the appellant. The appellant subsequently refused to assume responsibility for the respondent's legal expenses.

Decision

Applying Article 4 of Council Directive 87/344 EEC (the provisions of which are repeated in Articles 198-205 General Insurance Directive 2009/108/EC). The Court held that the appellant was not entitled to deny the respondent the benefit of her LEI. European Law clearly establishes the right an insured party to choose the lawyer they wish to represent them.

Mr Justice Longmore said in his overall conclusion:

> *"It is quite wrong that, despite the warning shot delivered to legal expenses insurers by this court in Sarwar v Alam [2002] 1 WLR 125 para 44, insurers should many years later be issuing policies which do not comply with the Regulations."*

The decision provides an irrefutable message to insurers against limiting the rights of an individual with LEI to select their own legal representatives.

(a) If there is going to be a dispute over liability, causation etc, and the case falls out of the portal, into the new fixed costs, it is well worth making more extensive enquiries as to BTE cover, and getting copy policy documents and calling the insurers to check, even if the Claimant says there is no cover, they often do not realise. Household, credit cards, bank accounts, car insurance policies etc often have BTE cover. Your clients will often not know, offer to send out an agent to check the policies and make the calls with your client there, it costs £100, but is well worth it, if there is cover.

(b) If Claimants do not issue cases, then Defendant litigation teams do not have a practice.

B) Alleged Fraud Exits From the Portal

Exit Points	How?	Section of Protocol in Support
Stage 1	The Defendant makes an admission of liability but alleges contributory negligence (other than in relation to the Claimant's admitted failure to wear a seat belt);	Paragraphs 6.15 (1) of the Protocol.
Stage 1	The Defendant does not admit liability; or liability is denied	Paragraphs 6.15 (2) of the Protocol.

Stage 2 Exit Points

- Where an offer made in the Stage 2 settlement pack, is withdrawn, after the Total Consideration Period. (see paragraph 7.39 of the Protocol).

- Where the second Defendant admits but then starts to investigate for fraud.

- Where the Court considers that the procedure is not appropriate (see PD 8B 7.2)

- Where a Protocol offer is withdrawn, after proceedings are started (see PD 8B 10.1).

- All allegation of fraud.

- Where an admission of liability/causation is withdrawn.

Other Revenue Streams Before You Issue

C) PAD Applications for Claimants

The Pre-Action Protocol.

RTA CASES

SECTION A

In all cases where liability is at issue –

(i) **Documents identifying nature, extent and location of damage to Defendant's vehicle where there is any dispute about point of impact.**

(ii) MOT certificate where relevant.

(iii) Maintenance records where vehicle defect is alleged or it is alleged by Defendant that there was an unforeseen defect which caused or contributed to the accident.

If a party refuses to disclose the engineer's report pre issue or photographs of the damage to the vehicle, consider a PAD application, if there is a dispute concerning causation, areas or consistency of damage, and then other side refuses to disclose.

Useful where:-

(a) The Defendant argues causation / LVI / no collision / inconsistent damage and refuses to disclose engineering evidence/photographs.

(b) Argue **proportionality** – better to have the engineering evidence pre issue to determine prospects – the pre-action protocol says you are entitled to it. There will almost always be a dispute in these cases about nature extent and location of damage.

(c) Ask the Defendant in open correspondence 'Is the point of impact agreed at …………..?". If the answer is no, ask for engineering evidence and photographs and if not disclosed issue a PAD.

D) Other Routes Out of Fixed Costs

See CPR 45:-

Claims For an Amount of Costs Exceeding Fixed Recoverable Costs

45.13

"(1) The court will entertain a claim for an amount of costs (excluding any success fee or disbursements) greater than the fixed recoverable costs ***but only if it considers that there are exceptional circumstances*** *making it appropriate to do so.*

(2) If the court considers such a claim appropriate, it may –

(a) summarily assess the costs; or

(b) make an order for the costs to be subject to detailed assessment.

(3) If the court does not consider the claim appropriate, it will make an order for fixed recoverable costs (and any permitted disbursements) only."

Failure to Achieve Costs Greater Than Fixed Recoverable Costs

45.14

"(1) This rule applies where –

(a) costs are assessed in accordance with rule 45.13(2); and

(b) the Court assesses the costs (excluding any VAT) as being an amount which is less than 20% greater than the amount of the fixed recoverable costs.

(2) The court must order the Defendant to pay to the Claimant the lesser of –

(a) the fixed recoverable costs; and

(b) the assessed costs."

There is no dentition of exceptional circumstances, each case will turn on its own facts.

<u>E) Fixed Costs Post July 2013 Part 36 Offers</u>

<u>If the Claimant obtains a judgment at least as advantageous as their own Part 36 offer</u> then, unless the court considers it unjust, they will be entitled to:

Their costs up to the end of the relevant period, presumably in accordance with the relevant fixed costs tables

<u>Costs on the indemnity basis from the end of the relevant period</u>

Interest on damages at up to 10% above base for some or all of the period starting with the date on which the relevant period ended.

Interest on the indemnity costs at up to 10% above base.

An additional amount calculated as 10% of the amount (damages) awarded

From a practical point of view in this regard, once a claim has exited the portal, therefore, it will be wise for Claimants to consider reasonable early Part 36 offers to encourage Defendants to settle.

Fraud: A New Focus?

Ostrach v McGreal and Others 2013 (Central London)

HHJ Mitchell dismissing 8 alleged Linked claims stated:-

> *"it is manifest that dishonesty was rife... I hope the message going out from this Court will be that if people lend their names to this kind of swindle they risk going to prison... I do hope that some publicity can be given to this case so that members of the public can be made aware of the consequences of members of the public getting involved, namely prison."*

And went onto give a warning to Solicitors:-

> *"[they] should think long and hard when there are no witnesses being called to corroborate the accident. This may be a pointer to the fact that the accident is staged and in my judgment it could be an abuse of process to proceed with such claims."*

What does this mean?

(a) The Courts are taking a far more robust approach to fraud most notably Central London and Birmingham.

(b) It is becoming difficult to win cases, especially in those Courts, without a very credible client.

(c) Claims, especially under fixed costs, will require early vetting from Solicitor/ Counsel to test credibility at an early stage. Early conferences with Counsel are now essential.

(d) The door is opened for wasted costs orders against firms / hire companies / accident management companies that pursue hopeless claims. This will become more prevalent.

(e) Early decisions on case are now essential. To protect your firm:-

i) Prior to issue, a statement should be signed and on file from the Claimant.

ii) The client should be seen in person (or if not by telephone), for a conference before issue.

iii) Signed statements should be on file from any key witnesses.

If not see: *Rasoul v Linkevicius & Grouparama Insurance* (Oct 2012):-

In *Rasoul* a claim where fraud was alleged collapsed at trial in what the Judge described as "spectacular fashion". A wasted costs order was made against the Solicitors because of the way in which the litigation had been conducted.

HHJ Collender QC who made the costs decision, placed considerable reliance on the following facts in making a wasted costs order as against the Claimant solicitor:

1. The Defendant insurer had placed the Claimant (and his solicitor) on notice at an early stage that they had concerns "relating to the bone fides of the claims".

2. The "unusually full" defence set out the Defendant's position on fraud "clearly and robustly".

3. In circumstances where the veracity of the facts in the witness evidence was being challenged, having the Statement of Truth on a separate sheet rather than in the body of the document was "a serious defect".

4. The collapse of the witnesses at Trial who abandoned their statements indicted "either extreme incompetence" … "or an attempt to establish a case on fabricated evidence".

5. The failure to obtain a signed statement from the Claimant or witnesses before the institution of proceedings where fraud was clearly

being alleged, was of itself evidence of incompetence (and therefore negligence).

6. The collapse of the Trial showed the weakness, if not inappropriate nature, of the claim and the collapse supported the early allegation made by the insurer from the outset.

7. Proper competent work by a solicitor would have ensured this case collapsed long before the trial that took place.

Fraud: Tougher Case Management Decisions to Come

Mohammed and Others v CIS (2013) Central London

The Court struck out the claims of two Claimants for none compliance with directions.

DJ Avent stated:

> *"There has been a wholesale disregard and/or avoidance of what was necessary and no real attempt, other than to pay it lip service, to comply with the unless order*
>
> *It is an undesirable fact that fraudulent road traffic accident claims are extremely prevalent. They tie up and use vast amounts of Court time but can be very profitable for the fraudster, particularly so if there is a multiplicity of claims by one or more Claimants. Fraudulent claims also undermine the integrity of the Courts and of justice generally. As Mr Nugent observed in his Skeleton Argument, where fraud is front and centre of the Defence, two clear principles emerge: firstly, that public policy in the administration of justice require that claims of this nature be properly investigated and deterred where appropriate and, secondly, that this can only happen if the Claimant gives full and frank disclosure. In a case where a Claimant is alleged to have concocted their claim, it is probable that that Claimant will not be willing to assist in establishing the fraud.*

> *Indeed, in cases where the first Defendant, as here, effectively disappears and takes no part in the litigation whatsoever, the insurance company, which is obligated by law to stand, in indemnity terms, behind their insured driver, will be conducting the litigation effectively blind and at an obvious and distinct disadvantage*
>
> *Therefore, where the Claimant's solicitors are on notice of fraud then, in my judgment, they have a positive duty to advise their client to render as much assistance to the Court as possible which includes the proper disclosure of relevant documents. In practical terms this is no more or less than the Claimant complying with his duty to further the overriding objective pursuant to CPR 1.3 by rendering that assistance. The disclosure of such documents is as central to the Defence as it is to the Claimant who wishes to rebut allegations of fraud. Of course, a Claimant in such a case may decide not to give this assistance but if he chooses to take that route then the calculus of risk must change"*

What does this mean in practice?

(a) The Courts will now be more willing to make onerous disclosure orders against Claimants where fraud is suspected (all previous accidents, medical reports and engineers reports etc).

(b) It is essential to check the Claimants's accident history before proceedings are issued, the outcome of any previous (or subsequent) claims, and be concerned about any claims that did not settle or where dropped by the Claimant.

(c) The Claimant should give a full statement before proceedings are issued dealing with any allegations.

2016 Update – Qader v Esure

The decision in the case of *Qader v Esure (2015)*, is not a favourable one for Claimant practitioners.

What was the case about?

The case concerns whether cases that start off in the Low Value Portal should be subject to fixed costs (FRC) under CPR 45.29A, when allocated to the multi track.

What were the arguments?

The cases involved an alleged induced accident involving a number of Claimants. The Claimants argued that the case had been allocated to the multi track and therefore should not be subject to FRC. The Claimants made a number of arguments:

1. The Jackson report did not intend that the multi track claims should be subject to fixed costs. The Court had available to it a copy of the report.

2. There were arguments under the Human Rights Act 1998 about access to justice and right to a fair Trial.

3. CPR 45.29A was never intended to apply to multi track cases.

4. Rule 45.29A and the overriding objective, given fraud was alleged, it would not be in the interest of justice to apply the rule to multi track cases.

The Defendant simply argued on its face, the rule was clear, and that FRC applied to multi track cases.

What did the Court find at first instance?

The Court found at first instance:-

i)The determining factor was value and not track = FRC applied.

ii) CPR 45.29J permitted a departure from the normal rule, where there were exceptional circumstances.

The Issues on Appeal

The issues before the Appeal Court were in three parts:-

i)Whether the DJ has implemented CPR 45.29 purposely so as to implement the Jackson reforms.

ii) In accordance with the overriding objective;

iii) Whether there was a contravention of the Human Rights Act 1998 sch 3 and EHCR Article 6.

The Decision

The Court found in summary:-

1. The purpose of the Jackson report was to make recommendations, and not rules and the Court did not have to interpret the CPR to implement those reforms. It was for the rules committee to implement those rules.

2. The nature of a low value case, even with allegations of fraud, would not offend the overriding objective.

3. CPR 45.29J provided a safeguard against injustice, and such an application could be made at the end of the case, and if such an application was to be made at that stage it does "*not dilute the effectiveness of such a safeguard*".

How should Claimant Solicitor's deal with cases going forwards?

There has been much hype in the legal press about *Qader,* and that it spells an end to cases to standard costs on PI claims in the multi track. There are a number of important points to note:

1. It is still only a County Court decision. Whilst it is a decision by a Circuit Judge, the decision is not binding on District Judges. The Court still has a degree of discretion.

2. The case was determined in relation to the RTA portal only. It is arguable it does not apply to the EL/PL portal.

3. The case will arguably not apply to those cases that have already been costs budgeted. The Court, it is argued, will have already accepted that multi track costs apply to those cases, and if not, exceptional circumstances will apply.

4. The case will only apply to those cases not yet to budgeted and/or allocated to track.

There are a number of ways Claimant Lawyers can deal with *Qader* arguments for the time being:-

1. If there is an allegation of fraud case, with multiple parties and likely to go over a day, an argument under CPR 45.29J, can still be presented at the CCMCC. The Judgment in *Qader* says "*if such consideration occurs at the end of the proceedings*". It does not say the issue cannot be raised at the CCMCC. The Claimant may argue that the Claimant's Solicitor (and Counsel), probably acting on a CFA need to know how much funding can be expedited on a case and whether they are likely to be limited to FRC (£2,655 plus 20% of damages) or not, and whether Counsel will be limited to a fixed advocacy fee for Trial (maximum £1,650 in the fast track).

2. Cases where the value exceeds £25,000 (excluding vehicle related damages) should not be started in the portal, or arguably they will be caught by this provision. (1) The 'Protocol upper limit' is—(a) £25,000 where the accident occurred on or after 31 July 2013;

It should be noted that the case is currently being appealed to the Court of Appeal and will be heard later in 2016.

Broadhurst v Tan and Part 36

Broadhurst v Tan; Taylor v Smith [2016] EWCA Civ 94 where the Court said that Claimants will be entitled to recover costs on the indemnity basis where they beat their own Part 36 offer in personal injury cases which no longer proceed under the RTA Protocol (and will not be restricted to recovering fixed costs under r.45.29B and r.45.29C). The Court said:- *"Fixed costs are awarded whether or not they were incurred, and whether or not they represent reasonable or proportionate compensation for the effort actually expended. On the other hand, assessed costs reflect the work actually done. The court examines whether the costs were incurred, and then asks whether they were incurred reasonably and (on the standard basis) proportionately."*

This case highlights the point for Claimants to make early Part 36 offers to settle, ideally pre-litigation, as this will put the Defendant insurer under increased costs pressure to settle.

CHAPTER TEN
THE FUTURE OF FRAUD INCLUDING CUE PI AND THE FRAUD REGISTER (UPDATED 2016)

'Flash for Cash'

It seems, that one of the new emerging frauds which was widely reported in the media towards the end of 2013 is 'flash for cash'. This may involve an innocent motorist being flashed out of a junction by another driver, and then the car deliberately colliding with the other vehicle to make claims for compensation. There are no reported cases of this within the law reports, and it remains to be seen how this type of fraud will develop over the coming months and years.

The Jackson Reforms

With the post Jackson reforms upon us, difficult times lie ahead for personal injury firms dealing with allegations of fraud. The Government has already decided to take fraud and implement a number of recommendation by LASPO, the Legal Aid Sentencing & Punishment of Offenders Act 2012 and this has involved:-

(a) Removal of recoverability of success fees and ATE funding from the Defendant.

(b) Introduction of a cap for success fees under the Claimant funded CFA of 25% of damages excluding future losses.

(c) Qualified one way costs shifting (QOCS) in personal injury cases.

(d) 10% uplift on PSLA of general damages.

(e) Introduction of damages based agreements.

(f) Part 36 changes with potential 10% penalty award for Claimants who match or exceed their own offer.

(g) Abolishment of personal injury referral fees from April 2013.

The only change that the Government has not implemented is the increase in the small claims track limits, discussed elsewhere in this book.

It could be argued that this may have some of the following consequences for alleged fraudulent claims:-

(a) If the Defendant alleges fraud and/or concerns about the claim, an unintended consequence of the reforms under QOCS is that the Defendant may not be able to recover their costs, if the QOCS escape provisions do not apply i.e fundamental dishonesty in the context of fraud cases.

(b) If fraudulent claims are no longer at risk of the Defendant's costs this may encourage more Claimants to "have a go".

(c) With the extension of fixed fees in more RTA claims, this may mean that the Defendant's insurers may be tempted to settle more claims, rather than alleging fraud or raising concerns about the claim, due to costs implications and the advantage of settling claims under the low fees in the portal.

(d) The abolition of after the event insurance premiums and recovery from the Defendant's insurers, Claimant's Solicitors may experience difficulty in finding appropriate cover to insure cases with allegations of fraud even with before the event insurers and this can raise questions of access to justice.

The Insurance Fraud Register

The insurance fraud register is a database run on behalf of the insurance industry. According to the IFR public website the aims of the organisation are at http://www.theifr.org.uk/:-

> *"The IFR is the first industry-wide database of known insurance fraudsters. It is the latest step in the ongoing battle against insurance fraud.*
>
> *The IFR is a robust, secure and effective tool. It has been developed by the insurance industry for the insurance industry to help prevent and detect fraudsters.*
>
> *The IFR aims to protect honest customers and keep down the cost of insurance.*
>
> *The Association of British Insurers (ABI) is the sponsor of the IFR on behalf of its members. The IFR is being managed by the Insurance Fraud Bureau in partnership with the ABI."*

The Definition of fraud is set out:-

> *"Any party seeking to obtain a benefit under the terms of any insurance related product, service or activity can be shown, on a balance of probabilities, through its actions, to have made or attempted to make a gain or induced or attempted to induce a loss by intentionally and dishonestly:*
>
> - *Making a false representation, and/or*
> - *Failing to disclose information, and/or*
> - *Having abused the relevant party's position.*
>
> *And, one or more of the following outcomes has taken place which relates to the fraudulent act:*
>
> - *An insurance policy application has been refused*

• An insurance policy or contract has been voided, terminated or cancelled
• A claim under an insurance policy has been repudiated
• A successful prosecution for fraud, the tort of deceit or contempt of court has been brought
• The relevant party has formally accepted his/her guilt in relation to the fraudulent act in question including, but not limited to, accepting a police caution
• An insurer has terminated a contract or a non-contracted relationship/recognition with a supplier or provider
• An insurer has attempted to stop/recover or refused a payment(s) made in relation to a transaction
• An insurer has challenged or demonstrated that a change to standing policy data was made without the relevant customer's authority

Provided that:

the relevant party has been notified that its claim has been repudiated, or relevant policy or contract voided, terminated, or cancelled, for reasons of fraud and/or it is in breach of the relevant terms and conditions relating to fraud within the relevant policy or contract"

Claimant Solicitors therefore need to provide clients with a warning about the register. In theory any client who had a finding of fraud, fundamental dishonesty and or exaggeration at Trial, may be at risk of being placed onto the register. This has very serious consequences for the claimant in that it will mean that it will be extremely difficult for claimants to purchase other insurance products in future or obtain insurance at reasonable cost.

Access to Previous Accident Database

Claimant Lawyers have long argued for access to the insurers database for previous accidents, CUE (Claims Underwriting Exchange), but this has been resisted by the insurance industry for many years. However, after a long period of protracted negotiations, the parties have finally worked out a way to give Claimant Lawyers access. Claimant Solicitors are now able to access the database and undertake a search to see whether the Claimant has been involved in any previous accidents. It is also dealt now within the Pre Action Protocol which sets out:-

> *6.3A*
>
> *(1) Before the CNF is sent to the defendant pursuant to paragraph 6.1, the claimant's legal representative must undertake a search of askCUEPI (website at: www.askCUE.co.uk) and must enter in the additional information box in the CNF the unique reference number generated by that search.*
>
> *(2) Where the claimant has sent the CNF without the unique reference number required by subparagraph (1), the defendant may require the claimant to resend the CNF with the reference number inserted. The period in paragraph 6.11 or 6.13 starts from the date the CNF was sent with the unique reference number.*
>
> *(3) Where the claimant has sent the CNF without the unique reference number required by subparagraph (1) and the defendant does not require the claimant to resend the CNF pursuant to subparagraph (2), the defendant must respond in accordance with paragraph 6.11 or 6.13.*

It is too early to tell how effective the system will be in reducing fraud in whiplash claims, given the system has only been implemented for a number of months and time will tell whether there is a reduction in fraudulent whiplash claims.

Points to Conclude

It has recently been reported that there has been an increase in accident casualty fraud, in other words pothole frauds, given the insurers are becoming ever better at detecting and preventing fraudulent claims and fraudsters are now turning to new types of fraud in order to bring claims.

It can only be argued, that the abolition of referral fees in personal injury cases are likely to reduce the number of fraudulent claims. It could also be argued, that the traditional model of a law firm where the Claimant goes to the law firm directly, is likely to decrease this type of fraud, given that the Solicitor gets to know the client at first hand, and it may be argued that this may encourage more Claimants to go directly to Solicitors' firms in their locality, rather than instructing a Solicitors' firm at the other side of the country where it is very difficult for the Claimant Lawyer to have direct contact with the client in order to assess credibility. It is arguable, that the abolition of referral fees for this reason, are likely to reduce fraudulent claims over time but again it may be argued that the impact of the Jackson reform may not become clear for some time in this area of work.

Nobody wants to see fraudulent claims and the only winners are fraudulent Claimants themselves. The fraudster who misleads the Defendant's insurance company and Solicitor costs the insurance company thousands of pounds which is unlikely to be recovered. The fraudulent client who misleads his own Solicitor obtains the services of a Solicitor by deception. An in-depth and open minded investigation at the outset by the Claimant's Solicitor will protect the Solicitor from the fraud if this is the case.

It may be argued that an open minded investigation should start as soon as fraud is suggested and this is necessary because:-

(a) If the claims are bona fide they deserve to be put in as strong a position as possible to prove it.

(b) If the claims are wholly or partially fraudulent the Solicitors need to know as soon as possible so they can take appropriate steps to deal with the client and stop incurring time on their behalf.

(c) If the client is bona fide but for one reason or another will be a poor witness then it is better to discover it earlier before significant time has been expended on them, and this is particularly relevant with reference to fixed recoverable fees.

(d) Early investigation is almost always going to be cheaper in the long run than running a case to Trial and losing or folding just short of Trial. Failing to grasp the net simply increases the risk of having to abandon a case closer to Trial and incurring the maximum amount of file time.

It can be argued, that a careful investigation in response to fraud allegation may satisfy the Solicitor that the witness is genuine but nevertheless casts doubt on the prospects of success.

Sometimes the Claimant may feel the pressure to continue where prospects of success are poor because the Solicitor threatens the Claimant with a bill of costs if he discontinues. The Conditional Fee Agreement will normally allow the Solicitor to terminate the retainer of a client who has materially misrepresented the facts. However this problem is less likely to occur where a good investigation has occurred at the outset of the case.

It may be argued that credibility problems in themselves of a non fraudulent source would not bar a Solicitor from continuing to act on a private basis where the client decided to pursue the case notwithstanding the prospects of success. In some cases it may be necessary to notify the Court and the other side of a finding eg. that a served Witness Statement is incorrect see Queens Bench Guide paragraph 7.10.4(6).

If a client did not want to continue to fund a case privately and continue on a Conditional Fee basis, where the prospects of success, for example are less than 50% the Solicitor may have the following options:-

(a) Terminate the Conditional Fee Agreement and if the case is pre issue, simply close the case and advise the client he may have to find a new Solicitor.

(b) If the case is litigated, terminate the CFA and allow the Claimant an opportunity to find a new Solicitor and then apply to come off the Court record as acting for the Claimant.

Evidence that a Claimant has not told the truth on the other hand is likely to engage the overriding duty to the Court, and to the other party so as to prevent the Solicitor from continuing to advance at least that aspect of the claim.

It may be argued that there are inherent risks for the Claimant and the firm in pursuing a case where the prospects of success are poor and the Claimant is at risk of a finding of fraud on the evidence and these may include:-

(a) If the BTE/ATE insurance is not kept informed of the prospects they may refuse to indemnify the Defendant's costs, if the case is lost.

(b) The Claimant could end up bearing the Defendant's costs personally. It may be argued that most ATE and LEI/BTE policies will refuse to indemnify if there is a finding of fraud or exaggerated damage or injury or that the Claimant has misrepresented the facts to his own Solicitor. It is therefore prudent that the after the event insurer is kept updated at every stage of the case and including any new material or facts which come to light which may alter the prospects of success.

(c) The Claimant could face committal proceedings for contempt if he or she knowingly or recklessly signs a Statement of Truth the Claimant knows to be false.

If ever one is in doubt, advice may be sought from the Law Society Professional Ethics helpline or the firm's professional indemnity Partner.

It is clear, that this type of fraud is on the increase, and we are likely to see an increase in this type of fraud continue. However, it is arguable that some of the Jackson reforms, and some of the cases post Mitchell with the new tougher sanctions under CPR 3.9 may discourage some claims, leading to better identification and detection of fraudulent claims, and the post Mitchell cases may strike out claims much more readily from Claimants who are not complying with their disclosure obligations, or generally complying with the Courts Directions.

It is clear and arguable, that certain Courts are now taking a much more robust approach to this type of fraud, and it is arguable that this is only likely to continue over the coming months and years. Insurers are becoming ever more sophisticated at detecting and preventing this type of RTA fraud, and it can be argued from both sides that this can only be a positive step for all concerned with this type of litigation.

Conclusions

It may be argued that the Government's agenda for whiplash reforms may be at an end for now. However, it does seem likely at some stage the following reforms will likely come back onto the agenda in Whiplash claims, if the Government does not see insurance premiums driven further by the current set of reforms.

The long awaited decision in *Coventry v Lawrence* did not see success fees or ATE premiums under the pre April 2013 system be declared as compatible with EU Law. However, fixed cost in clinical negligence cases are firmly on the government's agenda, and it must now arguably only be a matter of time before fixed costs are extended to all multi track cases, ending the hourly rate costs regime in virtually all personal injury litigation.

Whatever happens, Claimant Lawyers must continue to fight for a system that allows injured people access to justice, at a reasonable cost. Arguably increasing further the small claims limit or abolishing compensation in low value claims is not the answer. One does hope that the latest set of reforms, together with the 2013 fixed costs reforms will allow a stable system that Claimant Lawyers can adapt their business models to. The last few years have seen the Claimant RTA industry turned on its head, and it seems we are not at the end yet.

CHAPTER ELEVEN
HAYWARD V ZURICH (RE-OPENING SETTLEMENTS AND COMMITTAL PROCEEDINGS) (NEW 2016)

Hayward v Zurich

Insurers who settled a personal injury claim when they suspected fraud by the claimant would be entitled to set aside that settlement if they later discovered proof of fraud. When seeking to set aside a settlement on the basis of fraudulent misrepresentation, insurers did not have to prove that they settled because they believed that the misrepresentations (in the instant case, statements made by the claimant about the extent of his injury) were true; they merely had to show that they had been influenced by those misrepresentations.

The key sections from the Judgment are as follows. In the Court of Appeal, the Court had looked at the balance of probability test for fraud and said:-

> *"6.5* ***There is no special standard of proof for fraud in civil proceedings; the normal test of balance of probability applies, though of course in assessing the probabilities one bears in mind that fraud is an unusual matter****. In this case, the evidence, summarised above, that CH was not in fact suffering from the level of pain and disability that he claimed is so strong that it prevails over his innocent explanations. The probability is, and I so find, that CH was experiencing some pain both before and after the settlement, and did want it treated and managed; but at the same time, he also wanted the maximum compensation he could obtain, and to get it he was dishonestly willing to exaggerate his symptoms to the doctors, and to conceal his real level of ability from them and from the world, so as to give the false impression that he was not capable of heavy work when in fact he was. He must have been aware by the time of the 14 October 1999 surveillance video (at the latest) that his physical abilities were considerably greater than*

he thereafter represented to the doctors and his employers' representatives, and I find that his representations made after that date were knowingly false and misleading."

The Supreme Court said in relation to setting aside the settlement:-

"As explained above, the questions whether Zurich was induced to enter into the settlement agreement and whether doing so caused it loss are questions of fact, which were correctly decided in its favour by the judge. I accept the submission that the fact that the representee (Zurich) does not wholly credit the fraudster (Mr Hayward) and carries out its own investigations does not preclude it from having been induced by those representations. Qualified belief or disbelief does not rule out inducement, particularly where those investigations were never going to find out the evidence that subsequently came to light. ***That depended only on the fact that Mr and Mrs Cox subsequently came forward. Only then did Zurich find out the true position. As Mr Hayward knew, Zurich was settling on a false basis"***

"As I said earlier, it cannot fairly be said that Zurich had full knowledge of the facts here. *It follows that it is not necessary to express a final view on the question whether it always follows from the fact that the representee knows that the representation is false that he cannot succeed. As explained earlier, questions of inducement and causation are questions of fact.* ***It seems to me that there may be circumstances in which a representee may know that the representation is false but nevertheless may be held to rely upon the misrepresentation as a matter of fact"***

"The second issue (also set out in para 17 above) is in these terms:

"Under what circumstances, if any, does the suspicion by the defendant of exaggeration for financial gain on the part of the claimant preclude unravelling the settlement of that disputed claim when fraud is subsequently established?"

The answer seems to me to follow from the answer to the first question. As I see it, it is difficult to envisage any circumstances in which mere suspicion that a claim was fraudulent would preclude unravelling a settlement when fraud is subsequently established".

An Important point as made in conclusion:-

> *"52. Insurers may often have grounds for suspicion about a claim but lack the hard evidence necessary to prove fraud. To pursue an allegation of fraud without strong evidence is risky. If in such circumstances insurers settle a claim, not in the belief that it is bona fide but in the belief that it is likely to succeed, and if afterwards they discover evidence which proves that the claim was fraudulent, can they bring proceedings to set aside the agreement and recover damages for deceit? In this case the judge at first instance said yes, but the Court of Appeal said no, because in such circumstances the insurers were not deceived. The question which court gave the right answer is important, both for insurers and for those who advise personal injury claimants".*

CHAPTER TWELVE
QOCS AND SECTION 57 DISHONESTY AND UPDATED CASES (NEW 2016)

Fundamental Dishonesty – Section 57

The section was implemented by section 57 of the *Criminal Courts and Justice Act 2015* which sets out:-

> ***Personal injury claims: cases of fundamental dishonesty***
>
> *(1) This section applies where, in proceedings on a claim for damages in respect of personal injury ("the primary claim")—*
>
> > *(a) the court finds that the claimant is entitled to damages in respect of the claim, but*
> >
> > *(b) on an application by the defendant for the dismissal of the claim under this section, the court is satisfied on the balance of probabilities that the claimant has been fundamentally dishonest in relation to the primary claim or a related claim.*
>
> *(2) The court must dismiss the primary claim, unless it is satisfied that the claimant would suffer substantial injustice if the claim were dismissed.*
>
> *(3) The duty under subsection (2) includes the dismissal of any element of the primary claim in respect of which the claimant has not been dishonest.*
>
> *(4) The court's order dismissing the claim must record the amount of damages that the court would have awarded to the claimant in respect of the primary claim but for the dismissal of the claim.*
>
> *(5) When assessing costs in the proceedings, a court which dismisses a claim under this section must deduct the amount recorded in*

accordance with subsection (4) from the amount which it would otherwise order the claimant to pay in respect of costs incurred by the defendant.

(6) If a claim is dismissed under this section, subsection (7) applies to—

> *(a) any subsequent criminal proceedings against the claimant in respect of the fundamental dishonesty mentioned in subsection (1)(b), and*
>
> *(b) any subsequent proceedings for contempt of court against the claimant in respect of that dishonesty.*

(7) If the court in those proceedings finds the claimant guilty of an offence or of contempt of court, it must have regard to the dismissal of the primary claim under this section when sentencing the claimant or otherwise disposing of the proceedings.

(8) In this section—

> (1) *"claim" includes a counter-claim and, accordingly, "claimant" includes a counter-claimant and "defendant" includes a defendant to a counter-claim;*
>
> (2) *"personal injury" includes any disease and any other impairment of a person's physical or mental condition;*
>
> (3) *"related claim" means a claim for damages in respect of personal injury which is made— (a)in connection with the same incident or series of incidents in connection with which the primary claim is made, and (b)by a person other than the person who made the primary claim.*

(9) This section does not apply to proceedings started by the issue of a claim form before the day on which this section comes into force.

One can note with interest how the section is now being used by insurers in respect of low value injury cases. Whereas previously an insurer would have been required to plead fraud, in respect of such cases, the same is no longer true for cases issued after April 2015. It is a common misconception that fundamental dishonesty under section 57 needs to be pleaded, it does not. Insurers are free to turn up at Trial, see how the evidence comes out, and if the Claimant has lied under oath or has exaggerated a claim in some way, make submissions concerning fundamental dishonesty, to dismiss the claim and seek costs. Some insurers are also choosing to plead that a claim has been fundamentally dishonest from the outset and this is not just limited to road traffic whiplash claims but extends to public and employers liability claims.

There has been much debate as to what '*fundamental dishonesty*' means and one of the first reported cases that has looked at the issue can be found in *Creech v Apple Security Group Limited, Severn Valley Railway (Holdings) Ltd and Irvin Leisure Entertainments Limited (unreported) Telford CC 25 March 2015*. District Judge Rogers set out:

> *"Having heard the oral evidence of the claimant and the defendants' witnesses, I have reached, as I explained in my judgment, the very clear view that this accident could not have and did not occur in anything like the circumstances suggested by the claimant. Although I shy away in semantic terms in normal circumstances from the use of the word 'dishonest', in the context of the rules in this case I am quite unable to find anything other than this is a case where the case advanced by the claimant must, to his knowledge, have been incorrect. He must know that he could not, once my findings were made, have been right. This accident did not occur as he said it did, and he must have known that. In my judgment, that advancing of a case so plainly against the weight of the evidence, in the circumstances that I have outlined, can only be described as a fundamentally dishonest claim, and whilst it gives me no pleasure to say so, I am satisfied in the context of this case that qualified one-way costs shifting should not apply, and the second defendant is entitled to his costs as against the claimant".*

Against this context, it is extremely important that practitioners check and double check, with the claimant that the claims notification form (CNF), particulars of claim, schedule of loss and any part 18 responses, are correct (in accordance with the claimant's instructions) before they are filed and served. The CNF arguably, can be the most fatal document in a whole case, and one must bear in mind what the protocol says about this:-

> *"6.6 The statement of truth in the CNF must be signed either by the claimant or by the claimant's legal representative where the claimant has authorised the legal representative to do so and* ***the legal representative can produce written evidence of that authorisation.*** *Where the claimant is a child the statement of truth may be signed by the parent or guardian. On the electronically completed CNF the person may enter their name in the signature box to satisfy this requirement"*

It is therefore essential that the Claimant has seen the CNF before it is submitted to the Portal and approved it and approval is not just sought on the telephone. The Claimant Solicitor's client care letter should contain a warning about fundamental dishonesty and the consequences of such a finding i.e. QOCS will be dis-applied, the Claimant will end up paying the Defendant's costs and perhaps being added to the insurance fraud register.

QOCS: A Warning: CPR 44.16

This sets out:-

> *Exceptions to qualified one-way costs shifting where permission required:*
>
> *44.16*
>
> *(1) Orders for costs made against the claimant may be enforced to the full extent of such orders with the permission of the court where*

the claim is found on the balance of probabilities to be fundamentally dishonest.

(2) Orders for costs made against the claimant may be enforced up to the full extent of such orders with the permission of the court, and to the extent that it considers just, where –

(a) the proceedings include a claim which is made for the financial benefit of a person other than the claimant or a dependant within the meaning of section 1(3) of the Fatal Accidents Act 1976 (other than a claim in respect of the gratuitous provision of care, earnings paid by an employer or medical expenses); or

(b) a claim is made for the benefit of the claimant other than a claim to which this Section applies.

(3) Where paragraph (2)(a) applies, the court may, subject to rule 46.2, make an order for costs against a person, other than the claimant, for whose financial benefit the whole or part of the claim was made.

For any practitioners undertaking any type of personal injury work where credibility is often the major issue, and especially Low Velocity Impact cases, this is arguably becoming a major issue. A number of well known insurers have openly set out in the press the number of findings achieved under CPR 44.16. In the *Creech* case DJ Rogers stated:-

"There is, however, an exception to that if the court is satisfied that in relation to the claimant's case there has been fundamental dishonesty on the claimant's part. The problem is that there is absolutely no decided authority, or reported case, on what is meant by the phrase 'fundamental dishonesty'. It may be of course that that is because those matters cause difficulty very rarely, if at all. It may be that it is felt that a decision at first instance, once reached, is so self-evidently unchallengeable that there is no recourse to

> *appeal to the High Court or the Court of Appeal. There is an unreported case of His Honour Judge Maloney in Cambridge County Court on entirely different facts than those presented before me in this case. In that case, the defendant was able to show that the claimant, having been confronted with evidence as to how he might have suffered a fall from a ladder, changed his account of how he had come to do that and, furthermore, having done that in relation to liability, plainly deceived, or attempted to deceive as to the extent of his injuries, such deception being uncovered by video surveillance evidence used by the defendants. It is unsurprising in that case that His Honour Judge Maloney had little difficulty in deciding that there had been fundamental dishonesty on the part of the claimant"*

The case of *Gosling* was the case referred to in *Creech*. Another example can be found in *Zimi v London Central Bus Company 2015 (unreported)* HHJ Madge said:-

> *" Clearly, the adjective 'fundamental' is important in considering whether or not there has been a claim which is fundamentally dishonest. I assume that the word, fundamental, means something going to the base, something going to the core of the claim, something of central importance and something which is crucial.*
>
> *A few minutes ago, I gave a detailed judgment on questions of liability. I am not going to repeat now what I said in that judgment in any detail. I came to the conclusion that I was not satisfied that there was a collision, but that if there was it had occurred while the defendant's bus was stationary. Whilst perhaps out of charity to the claimant, I did not specifically find in my judgment that his evidence was fundamentally dishonest, I did refer to a number of issues of credibility. I am satisfied that this is not a claim which could have been brought in a mistaken belief. The claimant cannot have had an honest belief that there was a collision of the kind claimed. This is not a case in which there is any question of the claimant being naïve or unworldly. I bear in mind the previous claims of a similar nature, which he has made.*

> *Having regard to the matters to which I referred in my judgment and to the matters to which I have just referred to I am satisfied that the claimant's claim was fundamentally dishonest".*

Another useful example can be found in Zurich Insurance v Bain 2015 Newcastle County Court, where the Court said:-

> "***At all events, it looks as if Mr Bain succumbed to the temptation that*** *was put in his path and, eventually, he was referred to solicitors by the name of Clinch and Co. He formally gave instructions to Clinch and Co on 2nd September 2013 to pursue a claim for damages for personal injuries. They arranged for Mr Bain to be seen by Dr Mattinson, a general practitioner in Durham, for the purposes of the claim. The consultation took place on 19th September, eleven months after the accident. In that medical report prepared following this examination, it is recorded that the claimant was thrown sideways as a result of the accident; and that apparently he suffered moderate lower back pain which resolved after eight weeks.* ***He said that he had physical discomfort when driving and he was restricted in his ability to garden. When asked about his past medical history, Mr Bain mainly referred to osteoarthritis in his knee and hip and mentioned that he had had a hip replacement. There was, however, no reference to any previous back problem.*** *The report was attached to the Particulars of Claim which were served on 6 th March 2014. Mr Bain authorised the legal executive to sign the statement of case stating that it was true.*
>
> ***The defence made clear that it was not accepted that any injury could have been suffered as a result of this very minor impact, there being no risk of any occupant displacement****. Additionally, in the defence, a specific reference was made to the phone call with the Insurers. Notwithstanding that it was apparent that Zurich Insurance were going to rely upon what Mr Bain said in the phone call on 21st January 2013, the claim was pursued.*

So it was that it came in front of District Judge Goudie on 22nd January 2015. Mr Bain was cross-examined by Mr Paige, who appears before me, on behalf of Zurich, about the telephone call and about his previous back problems, as to which the medical records were available. I remind myself that the accident having occurred on 13th October 2012, on 16th July 2012 the claimant consulted his GP about lower lumbar back pain. The x- rays which were subsequently taken revealed moderately severe changes in the lumbar spine. On 21st August 2012, but two months before the accident, an MRI scan showed abnormality of the lumbar spine and the report of that scan is very detailed, identifying a large number of abnormalities in the claimant's back.

8. When Mr Bain gave evidence before the District Judge, he claimed he told Dr Mattinson about his back problems and that he had suffered a back injury. The District Judge's findings, as I understand them to be, (unfortunately the tape recording of the hearing of the judgment could not be located and so there was no actual transcript, though I do have the benefit of Mr Paige's written summary of what he recalls the District Judge said) were that contrary to what had been asserted in the particulars of claim, the medical report and his own witness statement, in fact, Mr Bain suffered no injury at all in the accident. ***By implication, he found that he had told an untruth to Dr Mattinson. He had given a witness statement which described in some detail the problems which he apparently suffered: stiffness, his reliance upon ibuprofen, problems with driving and so forth. Plainly, the District Judge rejected that written evidence as not being truthful and added to that, the District Judge found that Mr Bain had not told Dr Mattinson about his previous back problems.***

All those findings seem to me to be entirely justified on the evidence. For example, in relation to the failure to tell Dr Makinson about the back problems, it is inconceivable that if he had mentioned the back problems, Dr Mattinson would not have recorded that past history because they would have been

directly relevant to his complaints of back pain. *I am told by Mr Paige that Mr Bain sought to argue that it was only after the aches and pains continued for an extended period of time that he attributed any injury to the accident. However, as Mr Paige rightly points out, the telephone call with Zurich took place after the alleged period of symptoms had come to an end (being about eight weeks) and the telephone call took place about eleven weeks after the accident.*

Therefore, the issue which arises now on appeal is whether the District Judge was wrong in not finding that this claimant was fundamentally dishonest. It is not good enough for this court simply to come to the view that it would have acceded to the submission made on behalf of Zurich. *This court merely reviews the decision of the lower court. I can only interfere if I am satisfied that the decision was wrong or it exceeded the generous ambit of discretion afforded to a District Judge.*

What it comes to is this: what does fundamentally dishonest mean? It does not, in my judgment, cover situations where there is simply exaggeration or embellishment. It is not unknown for these courts to hear claimants who appear to have suffered injury but who, whether consciously or otherwise, overstate the extent of their injuries. Therefore, for example, commonly, a soft tissue injury of the neck or back may be said to be more severe than a court concludes it actually was. That would not be fundamentally dishonest. Equally, in the experience of these courts, from time to time, schedules of loss are presented which somewhat magnify the degree of disability, for example, exaggerating the need for help with gardening and DIY and claiming an excessive number of hours Again, generally speaking, I would not regard a schedule of loss, which rather exaggerates the claim for loss of services, to amount to being fundamentally dishonest. Having said that, these cases are fact sensitive and there may be situations where if a claim is patently and obviously exaggerated, the sole purpose being to recover damages to which a claimant is not entitled, it may be that a judge concludes that that renders the claim fundamentally dishonest.

Where I am quite satisfied fundamental dishonesty does arise is where it goes to the core of the claim. If the dishonesty is really at the root of the claim then it seems to me that the dishonesty can properly be categorised as being fundamental. *I test that proposition in the context of this case. The car repairs were paid for by the insurance company and it seems that the claimant was given a hire car as well. That being so, if, as the judge found, the claimant suffered no injury, there was no claim here.* ***It follows that this claim would never have been started but for Mr Bain's false assertion that he had suffered injury. It seems to me, therefore, that the dishonesty here goes far beyond mere exaggeration; it props up, and provides the sole basis for the claim. Without it, as I say, there would be no claim.***

It seems to me that in looking at the issue of fundamental dishonesty a Court is entitled to consider not only the effect of the dishonest but also the degree of dishonesty. I regret to say that I find that this is a very serious level of dishonesty for a number of reasons. ***Untruths were told to Dr Mattinson and important information within the knowledge of the claimant was withheld from Dr Mattinson. There was, as I say, a statement of truth appended to the Particulars of Claim which the claimant authorised and signed. There was a witness statement signed by the claimant which contained untruths. Furthermore, and I have already touched upon this, it seems to me that once the claimant and his solicitors were alerted to the fact that Zurich would rely upon the contents of the telephone conversation, it is striking that, nevertheless, the claimant pursued this claim and gave what has to be viewed as perjured evidence before the District Judge.***

For all those reasons, it seems to me that this is serious dishonesty and it is difficult to imagine a case where it is more central to the claim than it was here.

> *I conclude, therefore, that the District Judge's finding that it did not cross the threshold cannot be sustained on the evidence. If this is not a case of fundamental dishonesty, one has to ask when a claim does properly fall into that category. I therefore find that the conclusion of the District Judge was wrong and it cannot be upheld. The order that the court should have made was permission for the defendant to enforce the full extent of the order for costs. The qualified one way costs order is, as I understand it, a provision that is made in order to protect a deserving claimant from a costs liability that he would otherwise face. I regret to say that Mr Bain, for reasons which I have explained, is not a deserving claimant. I add this: I have no doubt that, generally speaking, Mr Bain is an upright and honest member of society, but on this occasion, he has left himself down.* ***I cannot simply take the view that because he has held high positions within the ambulance service that he has not been dishonest on this occasion****. I have to look at the facts surrounding this claim and, as I say, I have concluded that he has been fundamentally dishonest in the context of this case. Therefore, I make an order that the costs can be enforced against him"*

It may be argued QOCS is being used numerous ways for the Defendant to recover its costs and in must be borne in mind that this does not only apply to cases of fundamental dishonesty, but it can also can apply to other scenarios as follows:-

Exceptions to qualified one-way costs shifting where permission not required

44.15 Orders for costs made against the claimant may be enforced to the full extent of such orders without the permission of the court where the proceedings have been struck out on the grounds that –

(a) the claimant has disclosed no reasonable grounds for bringing the proceedings;

(b) the proceedings are an abuse of the court's process; or

> *(c) the conduct of–*
> *(i) the claimant; or*
> *(ii) a person acting on the claimant's behalf and with the claimant's knowledge of such conduct, is likely to obstruct the just disposal of the proceedings.*

The Claimant therefore cannot issue proceedings for cases with no merits or credibility concerns, discontinue and rely upon QOCS protection. It is open to the Defendant to seek to aside the Notice of Discontinuance, and ask the claim be struck out under CPR 44.15 or ask the Court to make a finding it is fundamentally dishonest under CPR 44.16. There are now examples where insurers are taking this course of action. Once upon a time the insurer may have been happy to take the saving of the success fee / ATE premium of pre April 2013 cases, but those days seem to be behind us, in such cases.

QOCS – An Exception

There is another case in relation to QOCS where the Court expressed a different view. The Court refused the defendant's application for permission to Appeal, where the District Judge had found a claim was not fundamentally dishonest, just because she had rejected the Claimant's version of events.

The Appellant Court said as follows:-

> *"His Honour Judge Freedman : This is an application for permission to appeal against a costs decision made by District Judge Charnock-Neal following a hearing of a fast track trial on 20th January 2016. In my order for today's hearing I directed that, if permission is granted, then the full appeal should proceed. In the event, I confine myself only to the question of whether permission should be granted at this stage. In order to grant permission to appeal there needs to be a real prospect of success.*
>
> *The trial concerned a road traffic accident which occurred on 28th October 2014. The claimant, Mr Nesham, was driving a Ford*

Transit truck along the coast road. The defendant, in the course of his business with Sunrich Clothing Limited, was driving a Mercedes. They were both travelling east along the coast road towards the coast. A collision occurred on the coast road between the front of the Mercedes and the rear of the Ford Transit. It was the claimant's case that, at the time of the collision, his vehicle was stationary in the outside lane of the eastbound carriageway and that the defendant had simply drove into the rear of his Ford Transit. In marked contrast the defendant said that the claimant had driven from a slip road onto the coast road, into his path, making a collision unavoidable.

The engineering evidence strongly suggested that the collision had occurred between the two vehicles at a time when the vehicles were at an angle to each other rather than it being a rear end shunt.

The only other evidence, apart from Mr Nesham and Mr Segal, the defendant, came from Mr Nesham's son. The district judge did not find that his evidence was of any particular assistance. ***In the end the district judge preferred the account provided by the defendant so she concluded that the claimant had not proved his claim and the claim was dismissed.***

After giving her findings Mr Tinnion, who appears before me today and who appeared at first instance, made an application pursuant to CPR 44.16 that the usual QOCS order should be disapplied and the costs order against the Claimant should be enforced because, he submitted, the claim was fundamentally dishonest. *The provision at CPR 44.16(1) reads as follows:*

" Orders for costs made against the claimant may be enforced to the full extent of such orders with the permission of the court where the claim is found, on the balance of probabilities, to be fundamentally dishonest."

The district judge listened to submissions about whether the claimant was fundamentally dishonest. Having reconsidered the evidence, she did not find that the Claimant was fundamentally dishonest. She said this:

"He gave me his version of events, I preferred not to accept that version but it does not necessarily follow that he was fundamentally dishonest."

And so she declined to make an order that the costs be enforced. It is her refusal to make an order pursuant to 44.16(1) which is the subject matter of this appeal.

It is said by Mr Tinnion, with commendable economy and clarity, that the decision of the district judge was perverse and secondly, if she was to find that the claim was not fundamentally dishonest, she failed to provide any proper reasons.

I start from this position. The district judge heard the evidence; she observed the claimant and the defendant, and indeed the claimant's son, give evidence. She was best placed to make an assessment of the witnesses; of their credibility; and of their veracity. She concluded that, whilst she was not able to accept the claimant's account, he was not fundamentally dishonest; indeed that he was not dishonest at all. Before she gave her reasons as to why she rejected the claimant's account, she said:

"It is clear that the claimant found giving evidence in court today quite difficult. I find that he was trying to assist the court."

It is difficult to see such an observation being, in any remote way, consistent with a finding that he was fundamentally dishonest.

Be that as it may, Mr Tinnion says that, nevertheless, this court should reject the judge's finding that he was trying to assist the court and that he was not dishonest. ***He submits that I should substitute a finding that he was fundamentally dishonest because it is ines-***

capable that he was giving an incorrect account when saying that he was never on the slip road; that was contrary to the engineering evidence and contrary to the findings made by the district judge.

It seems to me that in inviting an appellatre court to come to a conclusion as to the integrity of a witness, which runs contrary to the conclusion reached by the judge hearing a matter at first instance, is asking an appellate court to go far beyond what it can reasonably do, save in exceptional circumstances. Exceptional circumstances, in my judgment, do not obtain here. *There would have to be a good deal more than simply an account of an accident being rejected by a judge at first instance for an appellate court to reverse the finding that a witness was honest and substitute a finding that he was not only dishonest but fundamentally dishonest. There is, in my judgment, no basis whatsoever for coming to that conclusion in this case.* ***As I observed to Mr Tinnion in argument, up and down the country on a daily basis, judges are being asked to decide whose account of a road traffic accident is more reliable. And it is the experience of everybody who litigates in this field that drivers involved in accidents will give different and contrary versions of accidents to the extent of not just which lane they were in, but where they had come from, the route that they had taken and so forth. Maybe because they have a poor memory of what occurred; maybe because they have convinced themselves that they were in a particular location on a particular road or for many other reasons, which may not constitute dishonesty, far less fundamental dishonesty.***

And so, inferentially, this is exactly what the district judge found here. She said in terms, he was not being dishonest but I reject his version of events. She might have gone on to speculate as to why he was giving an incorrect account but she was not required to do so. ***As I say, there may be a whole host of reasons: impaired memory, or convincing himself, in this instance, that he had never gone on to the slip road, are but two reasons why an incorrect account may have been given.***

> *At all events, as I say, the finding as to fundamental dishonesty was quintessentially, if such finding was to be made, one for the district judge who heard the case. There is no proper basis here to invite an appellate court to reverse that finding.* ***Merely because an account of an accident has been rejected does not, to my mind, equate to fundamental dishonesty.*** *There is, as I say, nothing unusual about this particular case. It seems to me that the enforcement of costs must be reserved for those cases which are fundamentally dishonest; the district judge found otherwise and I take the view that this appeal, in such circumstances where an appellate court is being asked to overturn the finding as to assessment of a witness, has no prospect of success. Accordingly, I decline permission to appeal".*

Made in the USA
Monee, IL
13 September 2026

62975583R00085